John Steinbeck's Nonfiction Revisited

Twayne's United States Authors Series

Frank Day, Editor

Clemson University

TUSAS 662

John Steinbeck and Charley, his traveling companion, when he drove a pickup truck through about forty states to rediscover his country and his people.

John Steinbeck's Nonfiction Revisited

Warren French

University College of Swansea, Wales

Twayne Publishers
An Imprint of Simon & Schuster Macmillan
New York

Prentice Hall International
London • Mexico City • New Delhi • Singapore • Sydney • Toronto

John Steinbeck's Nonfiction Revisited
Warren French

Twayne Publishers
An Imprint of Simon & Schuster Macmillan
1633 Broadway
New York, NY 10019

Library of Congress Cataloging-in-Publication Data

French, Warren G., 1922-
   John Steinbeck's Nonfiction Revisited/Warren French.
      p. cm. — (Twayne's United States authors series)
   Includes bibliographical references (p.) and index.
   ISBN 0-8057-7831-4 : $22.95
   1. Steinbeck, John, 1902–1968—Criticism and interpretation.
I. Title. II. Series.
PS3537.T3234Z65 1994
813'.52—dc20   93-47472
                                                                      CIP

10 9 8 7 6 5 4 3 2 1

Printed in the United States of America.

For
Roy S. Simmonds and Robert DeMott, without whose constant encouragement
and assistance this capstone to four decades' study of John Steinbeck could never
have been completed

Contents

Preface

This book is intended as a companion to *John Steinbeck's Fiction Revisited* (1994), my third effort to supply an up-to-date critical study of this important body of American writing in the light of changing tastes in reading and criticism and increasing knowledge of the writer's life and works.

A problem facing the critic of John Steinbeck's life and work is that the quantity, diversity, complexity, and uneven quality of his publications make it difficult to accommodate a comprehensive review of them in a prescribed format. This is especially the case when, as in Twayne's series, that format is designed to reach those just becoming interested in the writer's work.

A major element as this problem applies to John Steinbeck is that he produced a large body of two quite different kinds of work—fiction (long and short novels, plays, short stories) and nonfiction, much of it about his travels, but some of the most important on the general state of his homeland. Since it was his fiction that first won him celebrity and that has continued to attract the widest audiences and most critical attention, most books about him, beginning with Harry T. Moore's and Peter Lisca's have been largely, often exclusively, confined to the fiction. This substantial body of work also offers—through a development that has been generally, though not universally, recognized as a false start, a quick rise to its greatest expressive power, and a decline in effectiveness—a convenient pattern for organizing a critical analysis.

The nonfiction offers no such neat pattern. Although Steinbeck began his professional career quite ingloriously as a reporter for a New York City daily newspaper, he had gone from his small West Coast hometown to the East Coast metropolis in the hopes of finding a market for his fiction in the nation's publishing center. Nonfiction always remained a kind of alternate career for him, to which he did not turn for important work or any substantial length of time. The unexpected success of *The Grapes of Wrath,* then the controversy over it, made him both an international celebrity and an outcast from his native culture, leaving him at a crossroads from which he did not feel could not proceed on the single path that he had so far followed. Then his alternate career as a nonfiction writer became a spasmodic one—a series of starts that were soon abandoned as he turned back to fiction until after winning the Nobel Prize for literature during the last decade of his life. Thereafter he completed and published no fiction but produced in autobiographical statements his largest and most comprehensive accounts of attempts to rediscover his native country and share his view of it with others.

In a sense all of Steinbeck's publications were autobiographical. Once late in his life he considered writing an autobiography, but he abandoned the effort. There are autobiographical elements, however, in his fiction, as in that of any writer whose stories are not purely formulaic. In Steinbeck's fiction before *East of Eden* (1952), however, his ideas and characters based on people he had known are so depersonalized or altered, often into symbolic forms, that they could not be identified until years later.

Since I have already discussed Steinbeck's fiction at length in my previous book, I have tried to make only passing references to it here. At times, however, particularly when there are long lapses between major nonfiction—or fiction—works, it seemed necessary to point out autobiographical and thematic connections between the two. I did not think that all readers of this book would be familiar enough with all Steinbeck's fiction to understand his sometimes abrupt shifts from one type of writing to another.

His first noteworthy nonfiction dealt with the plight of the dust bowl migrants to California in the 1930s, while he was collecting material that would be used in *The Grapes of Wrath*. Then he buried himself in the novel. Its success and the growing controversy about it led him to escape into other activities. He returned to reporting with two accounts of his travels. The first was about an expedition into the Sea of Cortez (Gulf of California) that Steinbeck financed to collect specimens of marine life with his friend Ed Ricketts; the next was a wartime account of three months in London and the Mediterranean theater of operations. These wartime dispatches, serialized in major newspapers, might have launched a longer career as a traveling reporter; but he was depressed by what he had seen of battle, and he turned down an offer to visit the Pacific theater and returned to writing fiction.

Then in 1947 he decided to pay a visit to Russia with photographer Robert Capa, the account of which was also serialized in newspapers before being edited into a book—*A Russian Journal*—to try to promote better international understanding. After it was published, he contemplated another expedition with Ed Ricketts that might have led to a new career as a marine biologist, but Ricketts' sudden death during a period when Steinbeck was having great marital problems led him to seek escape elsewhere. He plunged himself into research on the Mexican revolutionary leader Emiliano Zapata in preparation for making a film with director Elia Kazan. This project, however, disillusioned him with both Mexico and filmmaking, so that he turned again to a long contemplated novel about his childhood years in the Salinas Valley, finally published as *East of Eden*. In it he mixed scenes from his mother's family's life with contrived episodes from the longer account of a fictional family—the Trasks—of "symbol people." The mixture did not work well. Disappointed by the response to the novel, he produced between 1953 and 1956 the largest number of personal travel reports that he would write. Much of this material remains uncollected, like the most extended project, a series of essays about his personal discovery of Paris that appeared in the weekend editions of the Paris daily *Le Figaro* in French translations in 1954. Some of the translations appeared in *Un Américan à New York et à Paris* (1956); must have been published on the original English in American and English magazines. Although they provide some of the most revealing insights into Steinbeck's private thoughts, they have never been completely collected in a book.

Steinbeck's nonfictional works tapered off as he became more and more involved during the late 1950s in his attempt to adapt the text of Sir Thomas Malory's *Morte d'Arthur*, his favorite childhood reading, for contemporary audiences. He also turned out a few short novels and in 1961 published his last and one of his most complicated, *The Winter of Our Discontent*, his first and only attempt to use a fictional setting in New York state, where he had spent most of his time since World War II. Shortly thereafter he received the Nobel Prize for literature. The novel was not received with much interest, however, and, though he started some others, he never finished any. He devoted the last years of his life to his most ambitious nonfictional works—*Travels with Charley in Search of America* (1962) and *America and Americans* (1966), "a book of opinions, unashamed and individual," as he describes it—and two series of uncollected "Letters to Alicia." These he contributed to the weekend edition of the Long Island newspaper *Newsday* from 1965 to 1967, from his Sag Harbor home, Europe and Israel, Vietnam and other East Asian countries.

This book thus deals with an alternative career that the writer did not pursue with the consistency that might have provided a fascinating running commentary on his world. He turned to it with more than passing interest only during the periods after his three most ambitious novels had met with receptions quite different from what he anticipated: *The*

Grapes of Wrath, with an almost hysterical popularity that he never expected and did not enjoy at the time; *East of Eden,* with a lack of enthusiasm and understanding that nearly crippled him with disappointment; and *The Winter of Our Discontent,* with a lack of interest that suggested he had lost touch with contemporary audiences.

What is the enduring value of such a scattered group of writings? Does it help us understand an undeniable decline in his reputation? Some sympathetic critics have argued that there was never really any decline but that the change in Steinbeck's work after World War II resulted from his restless search for new forms. But these new forms were never as successful with the public or the critics as the earlier work had been. *Travels with Charley* was the best-selling of his books at the time of its publication, but there was a large audience with more money to spend for light reading in the 1960s than there had been during the Depression. Although the book retains a value as a period piece of a difficult era, it is rarely mentioned as one of his most memorable.

This book is going to examine the nonfiction works principally to advance the thesis that there was an undeniable decline in the effective power of Steinbeck's work after World War II, but that the decline was attributable not so much to changes in his views and expressive powers as in the times. After World War II, with the establishment of the principle of "unconditional surrender," the presence of nuclear weapons, and the engagement of the two major powers in a Cold War, there was a distinct change in the way people lived and thought in the United States, as well as elsewhere in the world. Steinbeck would not or could not adjust himself to these changes, so that he became a voice out of tune with his times. His fiction faltered because he sought to express his old convictions in new forms, but such formal experiments to place old wine in new bottles are rarely successful. After World War II, in many aspects of his personal life as well as in his writings, he is best envisioned in the terms of the forlorn ending of one of the few novels by a contemporary that he singled out as among the best in American literature, F. Scott Fitzgerald's *The Great Gatsby.* Its narrator, who has never felt at home in New York, heads back for the old frontier of his native Midwest, musing, "So we beat on, boats against the current, borne back ceaselessly into the past." (See "Americans and the World" in *America and Americans* for Steinbeck's summary judgment on the national achievement in literature.)

Just what this past was is best discovered by beginning with an essay Steinbeck wrote for the *New York Sunday Times Magazine* in 1953, "The Making of a New Yorker." In it he describes quite candidly how his first

attempt to settle in the big city in the 1920s had failed, but how, following his third marriage and permanent settlement in the East, he felt he
had made himself at home here.

He could have been wrong. Playwright Arthur Miller must have had
in mind this essay, published shortly after he met Steinbeck, when in an
interview with Jackson Benson, Miller established himself as the person
who appears to have best understood Steinbeck:

> I think what John suffered was really a personal thing. We have an urban
> civilization, and John was not an urban man. He liked to think he was
> sometimes. . . . And I think one of John's problems is the same as mine or
> anyone else's in this country or maybe in this world where there is no
> continuity, or very much community. He was trying to find a communi-
> ty in the United States that would feed him, toward which he could react
> in a feeling way, rather than merely as an observer or a commentator.
> And I don't know if there is such a place left in the world.[1]

Miller's sensitive perception of Steinbeck's problem should be kept in
mind during a chronological review of his nonfictional writings, particularly in light of how often these are concerned with journeys, quests for
some elusive grail, just as his and Fitzgerald's novels are. Despite the
diversity and discontinuity of these writings, there is an underlying unity
in their reflection of stages in a lifelong searh for community that moti-
vates also that restless voyager in Steinbeck's favorite poem, Tennyson's
"Ulysses," who "cannot rest from travel," "always roaming with a hungry heart," who has become a part of all he has met, yet finds

> . . . all experience is an arch wherethro'
> Gleams that untravell'd world, whose margin fades
> For ever and for ever when I move.

The problem of planning a book to develop the theme of the changes in
Steinbeck's life and work through his nonfiction is that the publication
history of these works differs greatly from that of his novels. Once he
had established his relationship with Pascal Covici as his publisher/editor,
the novels were published in the order in which they were written,
almost always soon after their completion. Much of the nonfiction, however, was not originally intended for publication, at least not in book
form; and much of it appeared only long after it had been written, some
of the most important accounts only after Steinbeck's death. I was,
therefore, confronted with the problem of whether to discuss the indi-

vidual titles in the chronological order of their composition or of their book publication (since newspaper and magazine pieces tend to become ephemeral). Since discussing them in the order of their publication after establishing the chronology in an introductory biographical chapter could only result in a collection of miscellaneous essays that could not consistently develop a theme, I have chosen in this book to discuss them in the order of their writing to try to produce a study of the changes and development in Steinbeck's interests, styles, and attitudes during a distinguished career of uneven achievement.

I could never have completed this book about Steinbeck's personal record of his career as a kind of lone ranger in a world he never made without the unflagging encouragement and unfailing assistance, over a long period of personal uncertainties, of two of those great friends who make life bearable and to whom this book is dedicated: Roy S. Simmonds, a retired civil servant who has become England's outstanding Steinbeck scholar, and Robert DeMott, one of the most dynamic and dedicated American university professors I know. I am particularly grateful to Roy Simmonds for immensely simplifying my research by sharing generously his own for his recently published *John Steinbeck: The Wartime Years, 1939–1945* (1996).

I am also deeply indebted to my longtime friend Thomas Staley, director of the Harry Ransom Humanities Research Center at the University of Texas at Austin (where I was awarded my Ph.D. in American literature and history for work that continues through this present volume to be profoundly influenced by one of the greatest teachers I have been privileged to know, Walter Prescott Webb). Dr. Staley graciously allowed me to examine the large Steinbeck collection now housed in Austin, particularly the correspondence between the novelist and his editor-friend-shaper Pascal Covici. Though not quoted, this correspondence is largely behind my formulation of the conception of Steinbeck as a last frontiersman, as presented in this book.

Chronology

1902   John Ernst Steinbeck born in Salinas, California, 27 February, son of John Ernst and Olive Hamilton Steinbeck.

1919   Edits high school yearbook *El Gabilan* and graduates from Salinas High School. Enrolls as English major at Stanford University, which he attends intermittently until 1925, when he leaves without a degree.

1925   Sails through the Panama Canal to New York City, where he works briefly as a reporter for William Randolph Hearst's morning newspaper, the *American*.

1929   *Cup of Gold* (historical novel).

1930   Marries Carol Henning of San Jose, California, 14 January; becomes lifelong client of New York literary agents Mavis McIntosh and Elizabeth Otis; meets Ed Ricketts in Monterey in October.

1932   *The Pastures of Heaven* (story cycle/novel).

1933   *To a God Unknown* (novel).

1934   Pascal Covici becomes lifelong editor.

1935   *Tortilla Flat* (story cycle/novel)—winner of annual Commonwealth Club of California award for best novel by a state resident.

1936   *In Dubious Battle* (novel); "Dubious Battle in California" (*Nation*, 13 September); "The Harvest Gypsies" (*San Francisco News*, 5–12 October).

1937   *Of Mice and Men* (novel and play); play version wins New York Critics Circle Award; chosen one of the 10 outstanding young men of the year; first trip to Europe.

1938   *The Long Valley* (short stories); *Their Blood Is Strong* (essays); moves with Pascal Covici to Viking Press, with which they remain affiliated the rest of their lives.

1939   *The Grapes of Wrath* (novel) wins Pulitzer Prize; elected to National Institute of Arts and Letters.

1940   Visits Gulf of California with Ed Ricketts to collect specimens of littoral marine life; *The Forgotten Village* (film) made in Mexico with Herbert Kline; film versions of *The Grapes of Wrath* (directed by John Ford) and *Of Mice and Men* (directed by Lewis Milestone).

1941   *Sea of Cortez* (account of expedition with Ed Ricketts in 1940, lavishly illustrated, first major nonfiction book).

1942   *Bombs Away* (propaganda novel); *The Moon Is Down* (novel and play); works with playwright Robert E. Sherwood for wartime Office of Coordinator of Information.

1943   Divorced from Carol Henning; marries Gwyndolyn Conger in New Orleans, 29 March; visits England and Mediterranean Theater of Operations as correspondent for New York *Herald Tribune* from June to October; involved in commando operation in Italy with Douglas Fairbanks, Jr.

1944   Son Thom born 2 August.

1945   *Cannery Row* (novel).

1946   Son John IV born 12 June.

1947   *The Pearl* (novel with film versions in English and Spanish); *The Wayward Bus* (novel); visits Soviet Union with photographer Robert Capa.

1948   Divorced from Gwyndolyn Conger; Ed Ricketts accidentally killed when a train hits his car; *A Russian Journal* (report of 1947 visit to Russia with photographs by Robert Capa); elected to American Academy of Arts and Letters.

1949   *The Red Pony* (film with script by Steinbeck, directed by Lewis Milestone); meets Elaine Scott in May.

1950   *Burning Bright* (novel and play); marries Elaine Scott, 29 December.

1952   *Viva Zapata!* (film with script by Steinbeck, directed by Elia Kazan); *East of Eden* (novel).

1954   Spends summer in Paris with Elaine and his sons; contributes weekly columns to the weekend edition of the newspaper *Le Figaro;* "Good Guy—Bad Guy" (*Punch,* 23 September); *Sweet Thursday* (novel).

1955   Buys house at Sag Harbor, Long Island; Rodgers and
        Hammerstein musical *Pipe Dream* based on *Sweet
        Thursday;* Elia Kazan films *East of Eden* with James
        Dean (filmscript by Paul Osborn).

1956   *Un Américain à New-York et à Paris* (1954 columns from
        Le Figaro with some additional pieces translated into
        French by Jean-François Rozan); attends Democratic
        and Republican presidential nominating conventions as
        correspondent for the Louisville *Courier-Journal.*

1957   *The Short Reign of Pippin IV* (novel).

1959   *Once There Was a War* (collection of World War II dis-
        patches to the New York *Herald Tribune*).

1960   Makes a transcontinental circuit with poodle Charley in
        Rocinante, a specially designed vehicle, from September
        to December.

1961   *The Winter of Our Discontent* (novel).

1962   Nobel Prize in literature; *Travels with Charley in Search of
        America* (reports on his autumnal journey in 1960).

1963   Tour of Europe with Edward Albee sponsored by U.S.
        Department of State's cultural exchange program.

1964   Presidential Medal of Freedom authorized by President
        Kennedy, presented at White House by President
        Johnson; Pascal Covici dies.

1965   Begins series of "Letters to Alicia" in Long Island
        *Newsday'*s weekend edition in November. This series
        includes reports from Europe and Israel.

1966   *America and Americans* (a nostalgic statement of
        Steinbeck's credo as an American, accompanied by
        photographs of all aspects of national life); second series
        of "Letters to Alicia" contains reports from South
        Vietnam and other East Asian countries.

1968   Dies in New York City, 20 December, after extended
        illness.

1969   *Journal of a Novel; The "East of Eden" Letters* (diary kept
        in the form of a series of letters to Pascal Covici during
        the writing of the novel *East of Eden* in 1951 in New
        York and Nantucket).

1974   Boyhood home at Central Avenue and Stone Street, Salinas, California, opened as a museum on what would have been his seventy-second birthday.

1975   *Steinbeck: A Life in Letters,* edited by Elaine Steinbeck and Robert Wallsten; *Viva Zapata!* (screenplay), edited by Robert E. Morsberger.

1976   *The Acts of King Arthur and His Noble Knights,* unfinished, edited by Horton Chase, with letters appended.

1979   U.S. commemorative stamp issued on what would have been Steinbeck's seventy-seventh birthday.

1984   Steinbeck pictured on half-ounce gold medal issued by U.S. government in Distinguished Americans series.

1989   *Working Days: The Journals of "The Grapes of Wrath,"* edited by Robert DeMott (diary kept during the writing of the novel, issued simultaneously with an anniversary edition of the novel, introduced by Studs Terkel).

1991   *Zapata: A Narrative in Dramatic Form,* edited by Robert E. Morsberger.

Chapter One

A Journalist at Heart

John Steinbeck decided to become a writer sometime around his thirteenth birthday in 1915, when he was a freshman in high school, after being encouraged by an English teacher (Benson, 22). He first tried his hand at short stories; but since he shyly mailed them to magazines under false names, he never learned how they were received. He gained some more practical writing experience as editor of *El Gabilan*, the yearbook at Salinas High School during his senior year. And he contributed a poem and two stories to the *Stanford Spectator* in 1924, during one of the periods he attended college without completing a degree. He did not place any work commercially until 1927, when a short story, "The Gifts of Iban," appeared under the pseudonym John Stern in the obscure *Smokers' Companion*, two years prior to the publication of his first novel. No other publications during the intervening period have been found.

In the autumn of 1925, he had made his first long journey, sailing from San Francisco through the Panama Canal and across the Caribbean Sea to New York. There, after doing some backbreaking work as a laborer on the new Madison Square Garden, he obtained his first paid employment as a journalist. His mother's brother, Joe Hamilton, a Chicago advertising agency owner with national connections, helped him get a job reporting for William Randolph Hearst's daily newspaper, the *American*. Although the editors protected him because of his uncle's influence, he was clearly not cut out for the kind of pushily competitive job that newsgathering was in the days most vividly portrayed in Ben Hecht and Charles MacArthur's play *The Front Page* (1928). This was before radio and television became the principal sources of news, when reporters vied for "scoops" that might justify "extras" that newsboys hawked in the streets. In 1953 Steinbeck confessed in "Autobiography: Making of a New Yorker," "I didn't know the first thing about being a reporter. I think now that the $25 a week they paid me was a total loss. They would give me stories to cover in Queens and Brooklyn and I would get lost and spend hours trying to find my way back. I couldn't learn to steal a picture from a desk when a family refused to be photographed, and I invariably got emotionally involved and tried to kill the whole story to save the subject."[1]

He held on because he wanted to impress a girl who thought he should go into advertising. She married a midwestern banker just two days before the *American* fired him. He couldn't find another job in the coldhearted city, so he decided to work his way back to California with a menial job on a ship. "The city had beaten the pants off me," he laments.

Jackson Benson maintains that "in the purest sense, Steinbeck never was a journalist" (505). But this judgment is too dogmatic. In a later aside Benson acknowledges that he was "a journalist at heart—he loved to be in the middle of the action" (793). The statements can be reconciled by recognizing that there is a difference between headline hunting and the now more important feature writing. The legendary reporter of old depended on speed, agility, and nerve—qualities in which Steinbeck did not excel—and moved quickly from one story to another, rarely looking back unless some persistent mystery was involved. Feature writers try to influence the way readers see things. Steinbeck was to show the ability to assimilate isolated events and place them in a context of past history or future possibilities that could be communicated to readers imaginatively, in a way that either won readers' hearts or offended them so deeply that they were outraged. What actually happened over the years is not that Steinbeck came back to the journalism that rejected his early efforts, but that journalism came round to providing a new outlet for his particular talents and a new career when he appeared to be running into dead ends as a fiction writer.

The Road to Fame as a Novelist

Steinbeck devoted the first decade after his dismal days with William Randolph Hearst's empire entirely to his ultimately triumphant effort to establish himself as a novelist. The story of his daunting setbacks during the Depression has already been traced in *John Steinbeck's Fiction Revisited;* here it is necessary only to recall that after years of increasingly frustrated work on two rather fantastic novels, *Cup of Gold* (1929) and *To a God Unknown* (1933), both enjoyed only small sales before their publishers went bankrupt. It was with the more realistic portrayal of his native valleys in California and their residents (1932) in *The Pastures of Heaven* (1932) and "The Red Pony" short stories (1932) that he discovered the road to a far greater success than he ever hoped for or even desired. After publisher and editor Pascal Covici discovered these works and guided the young writer through some devastating setbacks, he rose to the top of his profession only a few years later in 1939, when *The Grapes of Wrath* enjoyed the rare distinction for an American novel of becoming both a best-seller and an award winner.

Steinbeck had begun to move toward journalism, however, even before reaching the peak of his success as a champion of the oppressed and notoriety as the betrayer of his neighbors. There is nothing remotely journalistic about Steinbeck's first six published novels and story-cycles (besides those already mentioned, *Tortilla Flat* in 1935, *In Dubious Battle* in 1936, and *Of Mice and Men*, also a great success as his first play in 1937). All of these are nostalgic reveries about lost paradises and the fatal consequences of human overreaching.

A change is underway, however, with *In Dubious Battle* that led Steinbeck back to journalism. *Tortilla Flat* still possesses elements of sur-realistic fantasy, but with his next novel Steinbeck moves into closer rapport with his characters and his audience as victims and shocked observers of the world around them. While *In Dubious Battle* is not based on an actual strike, it combines elements drawn from several in California. Familiar and despicable villains, flawed heroes and grotesque situations are drawn directly from the same sources as those being exploited in sensational tabloid journalism.

This change to uncomfortable realism resulted from changes in Steinbeck's own lifestyle. From the time of his dejected return from New York in the 1920s until the deaths of his mother and father, before the publication of *Tortilla Flat*, Steinbeck led a reclusive life, preoccupied with personal problems. The novel about Monterey's ne'er-do-well paisanos living a simple life close to nature struck a responsive note in a public in the midst of appalling industrial depression.

Meanwhile his wife Carol had been getting acquainted with labor organizers who were circulating through the region trying to stir agricultural migrants into action demanding better working conditions. Through them, Steinbeck met Ella Winter and her husband, Lincoln Steffens, a leader of the turn-of-the-century muckraking movement that exposed political corruption in its magazines and books. Although Steinbeck disputed the Steffenses' defense of Soviet Russian policy as a model for a Utopian future, he sought to cultivate the good will of a celebrated reporter. Through this connection he began to meet labor organizers who had been driven into hiding and listened to their stories. He was especially struck by the experiences of the legendary Pat Chambers, which he thought he might develop into a kind of first-person diary. Although his literary agents prevailed upon him to distance himself from the situation by drawing on the material to create fictional characters and situations, his original conception was essentially journalistic. If carried out, it might have become a precursor of such "nonfiction novels" as Truman Capote's *In Cold Blood* and Norman Mailer's *Armies of the Night* during the postwar years.

Although on this occasion he abandoned biography for fiction, Steinbeck was moving toward a more realistic involvement in contemporary affairs than he had sought earlier. In his next novel, *Of Mice and Men*, he drew on personal observations again to create what proved to be not only a damning condemnation of American insensitivity but a veiled reference to authoritarian tendencies driving the world toward war; then he turned the novel into a play to share its message with even larger audiences. He and his supporters were surprised when it scored greater successes than any of his previous works, and it did lead him back into journalism. This time he did not have to depend on the influence of an uncle to get a job for which he proved not suited; now the publishers came to him. Although he had refused to talk about his writings before, he published an unprecedented explanation of his aims in devising *Of Mice and Men* as a "play/novelette" in "The Novel Might Benefit by the Discipline and Terseness of the Drama" (*Stage*, 15 January 1938).

Earning a Byline

Nine months after the appearance of *In Dubious Battle*, Steinbeck published his first bylined article in one of the most prominent national liberal political journals, the *Nation* (13 September 1936). The novel was by then enjoying better-than-expected sales for such a grim work, and the magazine evidently was aware of its recognition value when it echoed the title in that of the article, "Dubious Battle in California," a short statement drawing attention to the plight of migrant workers. What it would be interesting to know is who initiated this new departure for Steinbeck. Did the magazine invite the contribution, or did his astute editor and agents circulate it? Unfortunately, the early correspondence between Pascal Covici and Steinbeck was lost after the bankruptcy of Covici's firm and his move with the author to Viking Press.

The emergence of the once failed reporter as a featured journalist was to follow, as the *San Francisco News* had already invited Steinbeck to tour the migrant camps and write a series of seven articles about them for the paper. These appeared over the week of 5–11 October 1936 and two years later were collected by the Simon J. Lubin Society under the title *Their Blood Is Strong*, a pamphlet with a specially written epilogue by

Steinbeck. (The series in the newspaper had been titled "The Harvest Gypsies.") The pamphlet has several times since been reprinted, and Jackson Benson credits editorial writer George West, who arranged the series for the paper, with starting Steinbeck on the road to *The Grapes of Wrath* (295).

After this breakthrough, Steinbeck generally avoided diffusing his efforts in order to concentrate on his fiction. Nothing more appeared in major magazines or newspapers, although he did write at least one more piece, which resulted in his long-running feud with Henry Luce's *Time-Life-Fortune* publishing empire.

After he turned down an offer from *Fortune* to write an article on the devastating floods near Visalia, which he called "the most heartbreaking thing in the world," because he didn't like the magazine's audience, he agreed to do one for *Life*, probably because of the exposure it would provide to a large popular audience; but the magazine wouldn't print it. Jackson Benson observes that, apparently, "he wouldn't let them edit it and some of the language was too liberal for the editors to swallow" (371). Steinbeck persisted in his efforts to place this piece, however, because the floods had changed his attitudes toward his responsibilities as a writer. They were almost certainly the reason for his abandoning an already finished satirical novel and replacing it with *The Grapes of Wrath*, for which the floods provide the background for the final episodes. Even the *San Francisco News*, which had commissioned his work before, would not publish it; and he could finally get it published only in the *Monterey Trader* (15 April 1938), just a month before he started work on the big novel. *Life* did use the photographs that Horace Bristol took while accompanying Steinbeck on two later occasions (see Benson, 371). This unpleasantness led to hostilities between the Luce publications and the author that continued until the end of his life.

There was no time for any further side efforts, even if they might have influenced large audiences, during the agonizing months that Steinbeck spent writing *The Grapes of Wrath*, the novel that would establish his international reputation while making him many enemies in his home country.[2]

He was so physically and emotionally exhausted—not just by the effort required to produce his masterpiece but also by the storm of controversy it stirred up—that he was tempted briefly to abandon writing fiction for a less conspicuous and demanding career. He contemplated becoming a marine biologist; and his first move in this direction resulted in his first major autobiographical work, *Sea of Cortez* (1941). He did not return to fiction until, after Pearl Harbor was attacked, he was commissioned to do so by the federal government, urged on even by President Roosevelt. Again the resulting novel, *The Moon Is Down* (1942), generated a controversy that led him to regret his decision, though ultimately it strengthened his international reputation and influenced the decision to award him the Nobel Prize for literature in 1962.

Between the Tidelines

Sea of Cortez is the kind of sumptuous book that only an author with a tremendous following could have prevailed upon an indulgent publisher to produce. Had it not been ready before the Pearl Harbor attack and wartime cutbacks in publishing, it probably would have been deferred or greatly cut back in format. It may be described as Steinbeck's first writings about his own experiences to be shared with the public, even though as autobiography it is not very revealing or accurate—he still wished to keep his distance. In its original form, now a book collector's treasure, it consists of a "Log" of around 100,000 words, transcribed not from a single original journal but patched together from several sources. It deals with a voyage that Steinbeck and his wife Carol made with Ed Ricketts and a crew of four on *Western Flyer*, a fishing boat, into the Gulf of California to collect specimens of the marine life from the littoral— the land exposed between high and low tides. It is followed by color plates of the neatly catalogued specimens. Steinbeck wanted to publish this book to help establish credentials as a marine biologist. While he was then much in the public eye, even his name was not enough to attract many buyers of such an expensive and—in view of the novels his reputation was based on—esoteric book. It also could not have been published at a worse time than 1941, when the entry of the United States into World War II distracted attention from matters removed from the national crisis. Since the "Log" was published separately ten years later, along with a memorial essay, "About Ed Ricketts," it has enjoyed steady but not spectacular sales.

Whatever the reason for the slow sales, Steinbeck once again did not follow up a start that he had made into a new kind of writing and a possible new career. When he returned to reporting in 1943, he resumed the role that he had abandoned in 1925 as a correspondent for a leading New York newspaper—the generally conservative *Herald Tribune*, whose reputation he hoped might calm some government agencies' fears about his being a possible security risk. This time, however, his bylined dispatches were prominently featured and syndicated nationally. He had arrived as a journalist, though he found in Europe that he was regarded with suspicion by some experienced hands.

These reports were followed by *Bombs Away* (1942), a propaganda piece personally commissioned by President Roosevelt that Steinbeck banged out for the U.S. Army Air Force about its training of much-needed bomber crews. It is usually listed with his nonfiction works, but it is actually a fantasy about the training of a "typical" crew as a perfectly functioning team. It was also to prove the first of a series of Steinbeck's pseudodocumentary books. *Bombs Away* must be considered one of his least successful undertakings; and, to be fair to him, one must realize that he realized it would be substandard, since on this occasion he had for the first time succumbed to taking on an inappropriate job under patriotic pressure. Instead of struggling to create characters with whom he and readers could empathize, he manipulated stick figures at the behest of others to produce a much too idealized picture—a dangerous precedent for a writer whose best work took a highly skeptical view of painfully realistic situations.

Steinbeck had been led into this cul-de-sac by an involvement in the national preparedness effort even before Pearl Harbor. He had broken with his first wife, Carol, and become involved with a chanteuse ambitious to break into the movies, Gwendolyn (later Gwyndolyn) Conger, who would become his second wife; and he had planned to move with her to New York to start a new career there. Before he could settle down, however, he was summoned in September 1941 to a conference in Washington, D.C., which had been called by prominent playwright and later Franklin D. Roosevelt biographer Robert E. Sherwood, who had become head of the new Foreign Information Service, a unit of "Wild Bill" Donovan's Office of Coordinator of Information. (This operation would shortly become the Office of Strategic Services, many of whose operations were highly classified, and eventually the nucleus of the CIA.) Donovan offered Steinbeck a job. The novelist turned it down, but worked in an unpaid capacity on his second play/novelette, *The Moon Is Down*. This was another experiment with universalized "symbol people," about the people of an unidentified, occupied country resisting their invaders. It provoked a storm of controversy because critics thought it was not hard enough on the invaders, who were not specifically identified as the Nazi Germans. Subsequently he would also accept assignments from the Office of War Information (which would develop into the U.S. Information Agency), the Writers' War Board, and the Army

Air Force. He applied for military commissions, but they were held up by red tape during conflicts between various government agencies, some of which were courting his services while others were suspicious that he had radical affiliations.

Finally friends suggested that he go abroad as a reporter. He thought it would again be wisest to quell suspicions by working for "a big reactionary paper" like the New York *Herald Tribune* (Benson, 514). The U.S. military finally cleared him as a correspondent on 5 April 1943. During briefings in London, he contributed short pieces about his experiences in the embattled city during June and July. These began to appear in the U.S. syndicate that the *Herald Tribune* had organized on 21 June. In August he got to Algiers and was planning to return home from there without having seen any military action at close hand; but he was finally given a chance to visit the Italian front. He managed to get himself assigned to a supersecret commando unit of the U.S. Navy, which he was surprised to find commanded by a Hollywood friend, film star Douglas Fairbanks, Jr. (who remained a good friend of the family). Despite his noncombatant status, Steinbeck participated in several daring operations led by Fairbanks, who was the only American to have participated in the pioneering British commando raids (Benson, 529). Steinbeck was even recommended along with Fairbanks for a Silver Star, but could not be so honored because he was not a member of the armed forces.

The *Herald Tribune* wanted Steinbeck to remain in London until the end of the year, but he had seen enough and rushed home early in October. Since many of his dispatches concerning operations in progress had been delayed by censorship, he did not finish working over his notes until December, when the final columns appeared. These reports could have been the beginning of a much longer alternate career for Steinbeck, as he was invited to take another trip to the Pacific theater of operations; but unforeseen developments plunged him into one of the most depressing periods of his life.

Crisis

Although Steinbeck had displayed bravery during his involvement in the Italian campaign and had carried his assignment through to its planned conclusion, he returned home a shattered man. The years of 1944 and 1945 were to prove crucial to the shaping of his future. His dispatches from the battlefront had been received enthusiastically, and he could have proceeded at once to other assignments in his new role as roving commentator. He probably should have edited the European dispatches at once. Abraham Lincoln's biographer, poet Carl Sandburg, had become a good friend of Steinbeck and wrote in 1950 to Pascal Covici, "I am sorry that there was never a book of Steinbeck's newspaper pieces during the war. I clipped some that are still good reading" (Benson, 660). Collections of dispatches from the front, like those by Steinbeck's friend Ernie Pyle, sold well. A book of his own might have helped stabilize his personal situation and won him a new following, especially after the lamented death of Pyle in the Pacific theater left a void in the kind of down-to-earth reporting that the home folks liked.

Apparently, a collection had been anticipated in 1944. Peter Lisca, who was granted one of the rare interviews in which Steinbeck talked about his work, writes that one was ready, "but he was too disheartened by what he had seen of the war to prolong the experience in any way and decided not to publish it."[3] The war continued another year and a half, but Steinbeck had seen enough.

Jackson Benson is puzzled by Gwyn Steinbeck's complaint that "for one solid year after he came back from the war he had no sense of humor at all," but was "mean," "sadistic," and "masochistic," since no friends or close associates reported such a change (540). Steinbeck, however, was always shy and evasive and took his traumas out on his immediate family while trying to maintain an impenetrably placid facade with others. Comments to his college friend Webster Street in a letter of 13 December 1943, as he prepared to escape to Mexico, which had become his favorite retreat, offer insight into his state of mind: "I'm going to try to get some perspective on the war by going away from it. I don't understand it now."[4]

He paid little attention to military developments, and he accepted no further government commissions. In a letter to Covici in March 1945, he lamented, "I've done nothing but write testimonials for Red Cross, War Bonds, Merchant Marine, a bunch of crap but it must be done" (Benson, 566), a surprising comment from the author of *The Moon Is Down* and *Bombs Away*. His flight to Mexico at this time was not a popular move with his fellow Americans; the country's refusal to align itself with the Allies had bred suspicions that it was pro-German and harbored spies. Patriots took a dim view of those who went down Mexico way chiefly to have their tires recapped and gorge on steaks that were rationed in the United States. Nonetheless, Steinbeck enjoyed "doing completely tourist things," he wrote to Covici in January (Benson, 543). And he became involved in a deal to film a short novel he was working on, *The Pearl* (novel and film released in 1947).

When after two months he returned to New York with Gwyn, who awaited the birth of their first child in August, he put this project aside to dedicate himself to an important work he thought he had to do, though he belittled it to his friends and associates. Working in an office that Pascal Covici arranged for him at Viking Press, Steinbeck wrote in a few weeks a novel that he took pride in pointing out contained not a single word about the war still in progress: *Cannery Row* (1945). A tribute to his friend Ed Ricketts about their life among the lowlifes during the Depression, the book met with disapproval from reviewers, who found it inappropriate and frivolous during a national crisis. It proved to be the closing chapter of his greatest fictional achievement, the series of novels about the pastoral California in which he had grown up, beginning with the stories collected in *The Red Pony*. In writing *Cannery Row*, Steinbeck exhausted his reminiscences of a world to which he could not return. His great novels about underdogs' suffering had enraged many fellow Californians to seek bitter revenge on him and had alienated even the old friends who had shared these experiences before the spotlight hit them.

He might profitably have turned at this point from fiction to full-time journalism, but he would have faced the same problem: the post-war world would prove different from what he had expected, and he no longer had the advantage of being an unnoticed observer. He had not been able to assimilate the horrors of his brief but traumatic exposure to the monstrousness of modern mechanized warfare; he sought to turn back the clock and beat guns into ploughshares even when technocracy had won the day. As late as his final statement of his credo in *America and Americans* (1966), he remained unable to temper his vision to accord with quotidian reality. In the book he recognizes frightening expansion of environmental problems: "our rivers are poisoned by reckless dumping of sewage and toxic industrial wastes, the air of our cities is filthy and dangerous to breathe." He goes on to say that "the river-polluters and the air-poisoners are not criminal or even bad people,"[5] but simply careless ones who can be shamed into better behavior. He devoted himself to a succession of increasingly unconvincing novels, inspired by his desire to perform the high-minded educational mission that he thought would win the day when he might have been better advised first to examine the changing world as carefully as he had scrutinized the vanished one. But he was becoming too well-known to get close to situations that might expose vested interests, and he was moving in a society where it was difficult to keep in touch with the underdogs.

The undeniable change in his work that took place after the publication of *Cannery Row* has usually been regarded as a decline. Steinbeck
replaced the portrayal of recognizable people confronting problems common to a nation in distress with the manipulation of symbolic figures in
universalized situations. The reason for the shift has frequently been
attributed to the loss of his first wife and his closest friend, Ed Ricketts.
His subsequent departure from his native California has also been seen as
cutting him off from the places and experiences with which he had been
acquainted since childhood. These important events were, however, "outcroppings which indicate the condition," as he explained to a friend in
describing the role of the agricultural strikes in *In Dubious Battle*. (*Life in
Letters*, 98). Steinbeck wrote one of his apparently most confessional statements in his essay about becoming a New Yorker, but his longtime
friend, film director and novelist Elia Kazan, told Jay Parini, "Steinbeck
was a Californian, never a New Yorker. It was a great error for him to
leave the West Coast."[6] When he settled down in his publisher's office in
1944 to write *Cannery Row*, he moved back into the kind of private world
he had lived in before he became a celebrity. He did not leave it until,
against the advice of those who sought to protect him, he set out on his
quixotic quests on the road with his poodle Charley and in Vietnam.

After his novels were attacked by fellow Californians, Steinbeck
apparently felt himself most at home in Mexico, where he retreated after
his disillusioning experiences at the battlefront during World War II. It
is possible to single out one decision that materially affected his pilgrim's
progress toward discovering a challenging new role that could make his
work of greatest service to the community. This was his decision to aim
"to make people understand each other," as he had defined it in the letter to his agents apologizing for having destroyed "L'Affaire
Lettuceberg" and replacing it with *The Grapes of Wrath*. He turned down
a proffered assignment.

Early in June 1945, the New York *Herald Tribune* asked him to cover
the proposed war crimes trials in Europe. Jackson Benson reports that
Steinbeck wanted to take this assignment, which would have obliged him
to deal with revelations that would test his concepts of the innocence of
human motivations if society is properly educated; but he felt he could
not abandon the commitment that he had made to filming *The Pearl*, the
tale of a poor Mexican pearl diver's achievement of self-realization (571).

During the 1940s, between the completion of *The Grapes of Wrath* and
Steinbeck's settling down to write *East of Eden*, he was involved in three
filmmaking ventures in Mexico. The first of these, in collaboration with

award-winning European documentarian Herbert Kline, resulted in *The Forgotten Village*. Then, after finishing *Cannery Row*, he went back to California in 1944 and began work on *The Pearl*, a projected film/novelette—an enterprise that took much longer than he had expected. The film was not released until 1947, when it failed to attract much attention in either its English or its Spanish versions. The third, a film about the revolutionary leader Emiliano Zapata, in which Steinbeck became interested before filming started on *The Pearl* in 1945, ran into even more difficulties, to the dismay of Steinbeck's publishers, and was not completed by director Elia Kazan until 1951. It had to be shot in Texas because the Mexican authorities refused to approve the script, which portrayed Zapata as a self-sacrificing leader of the people. All three films were distinguished productions, though even *Viva Zapata!* was not widely distributed; the American producers were nervous about releasing a film on such a radical subject during the McCarthy Communist witch-hunts in Congress and failed to promote it. It has since won international recognition on the art theater circuit; but one thing that has to be cynically reported is that whatever stories Steinbeck had written about the war crimes trials would certainly have attracted more attention and influenced more opinion than all three films put together. After the *Zapata* experience, Steinbeck became so disillusioned with movie producers and distributors that he refused to become involved in any further experiments in a medium for which he had shown great promise and talent.

Behind his choice at this critical juncture in his career was an infatuation with Mexican culture that grew nearly into an obsession. He spent about one-third of his time during the last years of World War II in Mexico, a choice that was not any more popular with Californians and many other Americans than his portrayal of the society in which he had grown up. His squandering of what some regarded as ill-gotten gains on unfriendly soil could be viewed as subversive behavior from the patriotic viewpoint popularly exhibited during this period.

By the time Steinbeck went to Cuernavaca in 1945, he had even begun a story in Spanish that he hoped could be developed into "something like the Don Quixote of Mexico"; as he observed it was "growing into the most ambitious thing I have ever attempted" (Benson, 571–72). Something went wrong, however, and the original was apparently destroyed like many predecessors. What was to have been an account of American tourists visiting Mexican shrines was transformed into *The Wayward Bus* (1947), which moved the action to California, where a hypothetical cross section of postwar America is being shepherded over a rough mountain road by a fifty-year-old Irish-Mexican bus driver, Juan Chicoy (another J. C. for those seeking Christ figures in contemporary literature). Steinbeck had high hopes for this fable, and it sold surprisingly well; but few of his close associates or disinterested critics cared for this stylized allegory that reverted to the affected manner of his apprentice days in *Cup of Gold*. Jackson Benson finds the characters among Steinbeck's "least lifelike and interesting" (583).

Searching for New Directions

After finishing *The Wayward Bus*—for the first time completing a novel ahead of his own schedule—he did not proceed with a new book. Instead, in October 1946, he took Gwyn to Norway, where King Haakon presented him with the nation's Liberty Cross to show its appreciation for *The Moon Is Down*. When upon his return he couldn't get a new play moving successfully, he turned to the idea of taking a longer trip financed by a series of reports of his travels. The idea crystallized when he met the much-admired war photographer Robert Capa in a bar, and they agreed that they should go and take a look at postwar developments in Russia. The *Herald Tribune* offered them a contract and put together a national syndicate for the columns. This time the series was quickly turned into a book, lavishly illustrated with the photographs Capa had finally been allowed to take by his suspicious Russian hosts; but again Steinbeck did not immediately follow up this project with further reporting. By 1948, when the book appeared, relations between the United States and Russia had deteriorated as the image of an iron curtain seized the American imagination to the point of blocking out other ideas. Few American readers were receptive to Steinbeck's idea of trying to get to know the country that had so recently been their ally. Further travels would have had to be deferred anyway, for Steinbeck returned from Europe to plunge into a new series of personal problems that drove him once more into despair.

When he got back to the United States he was overwhelmed by a wave of nostalgia and decided to devote himself to the "big book" that he had been thinking about for some time, tentatively titled "The Salinas Valley," about the region where he had grown up. The story was not to focus on his own formative years, but it would be partially based on his mother's family. He decided to go back to his hometown of Salinas to research the period in local newspaper files, but, ominously, Gwyn did not go with him or follow him with their two young sons.

Steinbeck wrote to an old friend, Swedish artist Bo Beskow, that he was thinking about buying back "the old home ranch about which the Red Pony and many of my stories were written"; but he was not sure that Gwyn would approve, as she had said she would not leave New York (*Life in Letters*, 310–11). Any such plans were dashed after his return East, when he found that he needed an urgent operation for varicose veins. While he was recovering, his friend Ed Ricketts was fatally injured in a freak accident at a railroad crossing and died before Steinbeck could reach him. When he got back again to New York, in particularly dejected condition, Gwyn confronted him with a demand for a divorce and refused to let him remove his personal possessions from their apartment before a settlement was reached. The world that he had been seeking to stabilize by retreating into the past had collapsed.

Again he retreated to Mexico, this time for most of the summer of 1948, returning to California in September—not to the old ranch but to the little house in Pacific Grove where he had lived during some of his most difficult times in the 1930s and where his parents had died. He was broke, without the reference books and research materials he thought necessary to continue writing, and owed taxes as well. He sought relief in his enthusiasm for the film on Zapata.

While engaged in what his publishers regarded with annoyance as this distraction from the Salinas Valley book, he made a visit to Hollywood in May 1949 during which he met Elaine Scott, then still married to film star Zachary Scott. A romance developed between her and Steinbeck, and they were married on 29 December 1950. In the meantime Lewis Milestone's long-deferred film version of *The Red Pony* was at last completed. It was well received by reviewers but dismissed at the box office as a children's picture. Steinbeck tried a third play/novelette, *Burning Bright*, (1950) on the uplifting theme that all men were the fathers of all children; but this confusing allegory appealed to neither readers nor theatergoers, and it remains one of his least successful productions.

Steinbeck, pressured by his publishers, decided the time had come to settle down and concentrate on the big novel he had been planning. With his two sons, he and Elaine spent the summer of 1951 in a rented house on Nantucket Island, where he recorded his steady progress on *East of Eden*, one of his longest novels, intertwining episodes in the history of his mother's family, the Hamiltons, with those of a fictional one, the Trasks, in a journal that he kept in the form of letters to his editor, Pascal Covici. (These were subsequently published posthumously in 1969 as *Journal of a Novel*, his first extended autobiographical account to reach the public.) The Steinbecks returned to New York City in September, and he finished the long work there by the first of November. He was disappointed when for the first time his publishers decreed that the novel needed extensive revision and cutting. He had to spend another four months on the manuscript, depressed by the discovery that he was no longer writing with his old facility. After finishing it, he felt he needed a long trip abroad. He turned again to journalism, arranging to do a series of reports of his travels for *Collier's*, then a popular weekly magazine. The Steinbecks were in Europe from March to the end of August, returning home in time for the publication of *East of Eden*. The arrangement with *Collier's* had not worked out particularly well, because he and the editors did not seem able to achieve a meeting of minds. He was also disappointed that, although *East of Eden* became a best-seller, reviewers were not enthusiastic.

A Downhill Decade

The 1950s were to prove a depressing decade for the Steinbecks, as well as many other Americans, during this period when the young people were called "the silent generation." *East of Eden* and following fictional works did not restore Steinbeck to the revered place he had held among American writers since *The Grapes of Wrath*. He was increasingly grouped with William Faulkner, Ernest Hemingway, F. Scott Fitzgerald, and Thomas Wolfe as members of a great generation whose time had passed. By 1961, Steinbeck had published his last three novels. The first two of these, *Sweet Thursday* (1955) and *The Short Reign of Pippin IV*, were relatively short and lightly entertaining. *Sweet Thursday* was an ill-considered attempt to return to Cannery Row. It also provided the libretto for a Rodgers and Hammerstein musical comedy, *Pipe Dream*, which proved to be one of the gifted teams' few failures. *The Short Reign of Pippin IV* was a by-product of a residence in Paris in 1954. It is one of Steinbeck's best satires, although it has aged badly. *The Winter of Our Discontent* (1961) was his only novel about contemporary New York, where he had lived most of the time since the war, but it was not received enthusiastically.

These disappointments with his fiction were not adequately counterbalanced by advances in his career as a nonfiction writer. Although he produced a great many articles, they appeared in scattered places, and few have been collected. In 1953 his last contributions to *Collier's* appeared, and the magazine itself disappeared in 1956. His best-known travel report appeared in *Harper's Bazaar* in August 1953: "*Positano*" was a celebration of the beauty of this Italian resort that was taken up by the national tourist board for continuing publication in English, Italian, and French. Steinbeck also began writing affectionately about old cars in a trade publication, *Ford Times*, and began a string of articles in *Holiday*, Curtis Publishing's slick travel promotional, which would also run some advance material from *Travels with Charley* (1962).

During the Steinbecks' summer residence in Paris in 1954, he also wrote a series of articles, plus two short stories, about his discovery of the city, which were translated into French for the weekend editions of *Le Figaro*, one of the city's leading morning newspapers. Most of these were collected with some other earlier articles in *Un Américain à New-York et à Paris* in 1956, and this has become one of Steinbeck's most rare publications. Some of the articles have also appeared in the original English in British and American publications, but the entire run from *Le Figaro* has not been collected in any language, although the pieces provide some of the most intimate published insights into Steinbeck's views.

In 1955 Steinbeck also began a series of irregular contributions to Norman Cousins's *Saturday Review*. He continued there as an editor-at-large until July 1960, when he was disturbed by editorial tampering with an article on the school desegregation controversy. Cousins did publish some pieces about Senator Joseph McCarthy, but not Steinbeck's most widely circulated and admired satirical sketch of 1954, "How to Tell Good Guys from Bad Guys," which did not directly attack the witch-hunting senator but ridiculed his like in terms of western movie stereotypes. This was first published in the British comic weekly *Punch*, simply as "Good Guy—Bad Guy," in 1954, but carried its final full title in several American publications.

In 1956 Steinbeck agreed to attend for the first time both major parties' presidential nominating conventions and to produce reports for a syndicate put together by the Louisville *Courier-Journal*, whose editor he had met some years earlier while returning from Europe. These turned out to be droll sidelights on the gatherings themselves rather than serious political discussions. In 1957, however, he wrote for *Esquire* an impassioned defense of playwright Arthur Miller, who was being tried for contempt of Congress. None of this material has been collected, however, because Viking Press was not convinced that collections of miscellaneous essays were salable at the time. In 1959 Viking did gather under the title *Once There Was a War* most of his dispatches from the European theater during World War II. By then Steinbeck had begun to concentrate his efforts on his long-projected modernized version of Sir Thomas

Malory's *Morte d'Arthur*, which he worked on for most of 1959 in the south of England. He and Elaine considered this escape from the American scene the most enjoyable time they spent together.[7]

The Road Back

At the beginning of the New Year 1960, under heavy pressure from his publishers to produce a new major work after spending much time abroad, Steinbeck decided to embark on two new major projects. These would provide him with a choice between alternatives for the future after a decade that had left him largely out of touch with the changing American scene and during which he had produced little to enhance his reputation.

He planned to write a novel about what he saw as the moral deterioration of the United States during the postwar period and then, in this time of the Beat Generation, to take to the road himself to become reacquainted with the country and to report what he discovered. It might have been a better idea to carry out this plan in reverse order, but both he and his publishers probably felt that he had better reinforce his reputation as a novelist before taking a chance on another untested form of writing.

As it turned out, the book of travels proved far more popular than *The Winter of Our Discontent*, which developed out of a short story he had published in 1956 in the *Atlantic* magazine, "How Mr. Hogan Robbed a Bank," one of Steinbeck's cleverest pieces of fiction since *Cannery Row*. In trying to incorporate this wryly cynical anecdote into a complex morality play about a society that he was not thoroughly familiar with, he sentimentalized and diffused his material.

Although the novel awakened little enthusiasm, it provided an occasion for Steinbeck to be named for a long-overdue Nobel Prize in literature. The award stimulated an acrimonious controversy over whether he deserved it, with the opposition case summed up in Arthur Mizener's sardonic meditation for the *New York Times*, "Does a Moral Vision of the Thirties Deserve a Nobel Prize?"(9 December 1962). Even sympathizers, however, seemed to agree that Steinbeck was past his prime and that the award was a pious rectification of a past error. *Travels with Charley in Search of America* tremendously surprised everyone, as Steinbeck, having been written off, returned to the market, with one of his most popular works. It sold more copies during its first months than any of his previous works, even *The Grapes of Wrath*, since it was offered to a much larger and more prosperous public.

The book was almost not written, because all of Steinbeck's trusted advisers, even Elaine, tried to dissuade him from embarking on such an arduous undertaking now that he was nearly sixty and had already had some serious medical problems. He persisted, however, in working out what he considered a suitable vehicle for such a junket, which he described as "a three quarter ton pick-up truck, capable of going anywhere under possibly rigorous condition," on which he wanted "a little house built like the cabin of a small boat." When an unspecified "great corporation" supplied "exactly" what he specified,[8] he named it *Rocinante* after Don Quixote's horse. He planned to depart after Labor Day when summer tourists would be off the road.

His departure was delayed by Hurricane Donna, which struck Sag Harbor directly just as he was about to set out. His vehicle was not damaged, however, and he was able to leave on 23 September on a trip through New England and New York, across the Midwest and through Montana to Seattle, where Elaine joined him for the trip home to California. When she flew ahead to visit her native Texas, he became lonely and hurried to meet her for Thanksgiving. Then he backtracked to New Orleans alone, where at the time of the confrontations over school desegregation he found the makings of a powerful climax to his experiences in the behavior of the "Cheerleaders," a group of white women determined to use the vilest possible tactics to keep one little black girl out of a previously all-white school. He was so shaken by what he saw and the conversations he had about it that he hurried across the South to get home for the holidays.

After recovering at home from more startling experiences than he had bargained for, he took Elaine to John Kennedy's inauguration as president in January 1961, an event that brought the progressive spirit of the American frontier briefly back to life—before the destruction of the new Camelot. During these promising days, Steinbeck appeared to have hit on a new career with the account of these travels that would get him back in touch with a homeland he found he no longer knew. The book proved a difficult act to follow. Although he had demonstrated that he could to some extent reestablish his connections with the American public, another troubling change came over the country following John Kennedy's assassination and the country's increasing involvement in Vietnam. This change was to have some calamitous implications for Steinbeck's last years.

Steinbeck had been closely associated with high-level Democratic Party politics since he had been invited secretly to contribute ideas to

President Roosevelt's fourth campaign in 1944, and he had been active as a speechwriter during the two unsuccessful campaigns of Adlai Stevenson, the politician that he admired the most. He had been more cautious about endorsing the brash young man from Massachusetts, but John F. Kennedy did invite him to the first presidential inauguration he attended, and later, after Steinbeck recovered from a serious eye operation, he set off at Kennedy's invitation on a government-sponsored cultural mission, along with playwright Edward Albee. While he was off on this trip, President Kennedy was assassinated. Jacqueline Kennedy thought that Steinbeck was the person best suited to write her husband's biography. He felt that he could not flatly refuse, but he delayed an answer because he did not think he could undertake the considerable research that would be involved (Benson, 949–50).

He became most closely associated with Kennedy's successor, Lyndon B. Johnson. Elaine had gone to school with Lady Bird Johnson, and Johnson welcomed Steinbeck's support, so that the Steinbecks became frequent visitors at the White House and Camp David. During the summer of 1964, before Johnson was swept to a landslide victory over Barry Goldwater in the November election, the president conferred on Steinbeck the Medal of Freedom, the highest government honor to a civilian in peacetime, for which he had been selected by President Kennedy.

Vietnam was to be Johnson's undoing and, to a certain extent, Steinbeck's. The United States became much more divided than it had been during the McCarthy witch-hunts, possibly more than at any time since the Civil War, as hundreds of young men left the country for Canada and Europe—some never to return—and thousands more remained at home to find other ways of dodging the draft and to hold massive protest demonstrations, at some of which draft cards and American flags were burned. Steinbeck was placed in a difficult position when, at the time of Adlai Stevenson's death in July 1965, President Johnson invited the writer to Camp David and asked him to serve as his personal emissary to Vietnam to bring a confidential report directly back to him. As Jackson Benson explains, "Steinbeck never adopted a political position because it was fashionable, nor did he ever modify a stand because it had become unpopular" (956); but, on the other hand, "the last thing in the world he wanted to do was to go to Vietnam, especially as an emissary of the President" (971). If he supported him, it must be as an independent.

He was able to forestall a decision temporarily by his work on what would be his last published book during his lifetime. *America and*

Americans (1966) started out as a collection of pictures commissioned from noted photographers by Viking Press. Their charge was capture images from across the country that would recall the traditions and natural beauty of the land in a time of distress. Viking asked Steinbeck to write a brief introduction and a set of captions. He accepted the task as a diversion to be finished up in a few weeks, but as he got into the project, he found it would give him an opportunity to expand on many subjects that he would have liked to bring up in *Travels with Charley* but that were unsuitable to its format (Benson, 955). The new book became one of his most intimate accounts of his personal feelings, presenting his considered judgment on the American experience from the nation's colonial beginnings. It is the most essential reading for an understanding of John Steinbeck as a citizen and a writer. Because the popularity of President Johnson and his supporters was plummeting when it appeared, and because it resembled in format the sumptuous Christmas gift books that flood the market every autumn, it was not taken as seriously as it should have been. It is the work that also accidentally consolidated Steinbeck's talents and achievements as a nonfiction writer. It is regrettable that he had not on earlier occasions been moved to pull together a statement about a changing society with the seriousness and dignity of this one.

This magisterial if sometimes naively old-fashioned credo was not to be Steinbeck's last word to the world. He was not to avoid Vietnam. As he was finishing work on *America and Americans* in 1965, Harry F. Guggenheim, publisher of the Long Island newspaper *Newsday*, enticed Steinbeck to follow up in his role of commentator with a syndicated column of reports that would help pay for a projected trip to Europe to continue work on his Malory book. This was to develop into Steinbeck's largest body of related nonfiction pieces, although the columns have not been collected. It would also be his last undertaking he would continue until his terminal illnesses, for which these strenuous efforts were in some measure responsible. It would also involve him in dangers and controversies that would blight his last days.

There was a macabre, funereal tone to the whole project from its inception when Steinbeck decided to cast the series into the form of "Letters to Alicia," Guggenheim's dead wife, who had founded *Newsday* in 1940. The letters began to appear in November 1965. At first they were rather superficial and somewhat sardonic comments on the political scene; but painful trouble developed early when Steinbeck's overenthusiastic report about the discovery of some Malory manuscripts led to a break in relations between Steinbeck and the distinguished Malory scholar Eugene Vinaver, whom the writer greatly respected. Steinbeck was to have returned home in January 1966, but his trip and the first series of letters were protracted when Harry Guggenheim suggested that Steinbeck pay his first visit to Israel. Steinbeck was most enthusiastic about the brave history of the ancient Hebrews and the way their descendants had made the desert bloom. As Jay Parini comments, however, "One must note, of course, his naivete in swallowing the Israeli Tourist Board version of Israel history without even noticing that the Israelis in their quest for statehood, had displaced millions of Palestinians" (563–64).

Steinbeck returned home in March 1966, but the columns continued to appear until May. An effort to get a new novel going sputtered out, and in November he concocted an agreement with the Russian poet Yvgeny Yevtushenko—who was visiting the United States after having attacked some of Steinbeck's views supporting President Johnson's policies in Vietnam—to make a joint trip through both North and South Vietnam. The Russian found the trip inconvenient for unexplained reasons, though Steinbeck thought them obvious. Steinbeck was also not granted permission to visit North Vietnam, Cambodia, or China.

He determined to go anyway, but as a correspondent for *Newsday*, not a presidential envoy. He did not even inform Lyndon Johnson of the trip until he was on his way, though he did make a personal report to the president when he returned. The second series of "Letters to Alicia," which appeared from December 1966 through May 1967, concerned his six weeks in Vietnam in December 1966 and January 1967 and subsequent short visits in Thailand, Laos, Indonesia, and Hong Kong. Both he and Elaine, who accompanied him on all but the most risky visits with troops in the field, escaped from the war zone without injury. Ironically, during the visit to Hong Kong in April, before coming home, Steinbeck slipped a spinal disc trying to help a Chinese workman pull a handtruck of beer upstairs. This charitable impulse set in motion a train of complications that led to his death a year and a half later on 20 December 1968, the Malory modernization unfinished.

It is additionally ironic and yet perhaps characteristically inevitable that Steinbeck's last major writings, his most ambitious reporting, should have dealt with the two great failures of his life—his effort to make his beloved *Morte d'Arthur* accessible to young readers and his attempt to vindicate the president with whom he conspicuously associated himself after shunning the spotlight most of his life. What he had completed of his work on Malory was published, but not by the house with which he had been associated through most of his career, and it attracted little notice. The "Letters to Alicia" crumble away in old newsprint, yet they provide unique insights into a time that should not be forgotten, much as many would like to forget it. Steinbeck's personal history does not really end; it just stops, reminding us once again of his favorite poem, Tennyson's "Ulysses," with whose titular monologuist John Steinbeck could certainly identify himself as one who has become "a name . . . for always roaming with a hungry heart."

Chapter Two

Discovering a Mission

Steinbeck's debut as a contributor to a national magazine in the summer of 1936 was surprisingly inconspicuous in view of the attention that his fiction was already attracting. The *Nation* (with the *New Republic*, one of the two leading liberal political weeklies in the United States) carried well buried in its 13 September issue "Dubious Battle in California," an approximately 1,500-word explanation of the historical development of the use of migrant agricultural workers in the state. It was Steinbeck's first nationally circulated statement of his concern about the unhappy situation of the refugees from the southwestern dust bowl.

The appearance of the short piece in this particular journal has not been explained in any published accounts. Did the magazine commission it on the strength of the interest and controversy generated by the recently published *In Dubious Battle*, or did Steinbeck's agents circulate it to call continuing attention to the novel? Records of the early correspondence between Steinbeck and his editor, Pascal Covici, were lost when Covici's publishing house went bankrupt and he moved to Viking Press. Was the journal trying to compensate in some measure for Mary McCarthy's scathing review of the novel some months earlier in a March issue? Steinbeck's work never appeared in the *Nation* again.

The only certain thing is that the article resulted from Steinbeck's tour of migrant camps during the summer of 1936, during which he met Tom Collins, to whom, along with his first wife, Carol, Steinbeck dedicated *The Grapes of Wrath*. This article was only a preliminary to the series that would appear 5–12 October 1936 in the *San Francisco News*, the first extensive journalistic reporting to carry Steinbeck's byline.

The *Nation* article marked a total departure from anything that Steinbeck had published before. For one thing, it pleaded for an amelioration of present conditions and expressed hopes for a better world to come, concluding, "It is to be fervently hoped that the great group of migrant workers so necessary to the harvesting of California's crops may be given the right to live decently."[1] This idealistic vision was drastically different from the apocalyptic one that concluded his three most recent novels.

Even though *Of Mice and Men* was not published until spring 1937, he had completed it the preceding August. This was just before he set off on the trip to the migrant camps with officials from the National Resettlement Administration at the request of George West, chief editorial writer for the *San Francisco News*. His observations during this trip had a profound influence on the vision informing Steinbeck's fiction. *Of Mice and Men* was the last work of a novelist writing in seclusion from an appalling reality that he realized demanded immediate action. The three novels written before this realization—(*Tortilla Flat, In Dubious Battle, Of Mice and Men*)—had chronicled the grim odysseys of young men with powerful imaginations and great ambitions to fulfill their dreams (much like Steinbeck himself) who are destroyed by inimical forces beyond their control.

All three innocents are doomed to the fate spelled out by the world-weary pirate-turned-governor Sir Henry Morgan in Steinbeck's first novel, *Cup of Gold,* as he condemns some former cohorts to death: "Civilization will split up a character, and he who refuses to split goes under"[2]—a viewpoint that darkly dominated all of Steinbeck's fiction before *The Grapes of Wrath.*

Inconspicuous as "Dubious Battle in California" was, with its rather stereotyped phrasing, it marked a turning point of great importance in the writer's life and work. He emerges here no longer as the resigned prophet of doom but as a reporter whose eyes have been opened to something he must try to make others understand. The article is not another sensational exposé but a plea to the country to amend its continuing on pattern of neglect. While what he describes is "news of the day" many would prefer not to hear, it is not just the news of one day. It is an attempt to put this news in a context that demands continued observation and action.

Steinbeck was clearly having a problem, however, in finding the proper tone for a kind of writing that he had not so far practiced. The article begins like a textbook example of the long-familiar first principles of journalism. The first twelve-word sentence supplies the information traditionally required of a news story: who and where (California's agriculturists), what (have experienced a revolution), when (over sixty years)—while the next two of eight words each answer the crucial why?—"Once its principal products were hay and cattle. Today fruits and vegetables are its most profitable crops." All this in the tense telegraphic style usually associated with Ernest Hemingway. These simple sentences are quickly replaced by more complex ones as the writer devotes the three brief opening paragraphs to establishing the nature of the migrant labor problems in California. He tries to keep the text impersonal, but attempting to avoid controversy proves too limiting, as his introduction concludes that the associated farmers of California have as their major activity "resistance to any attempt of farm labor to organize." Steinbeck still struggles to remain impersonal as he traces the use of migrant labor from the completion of the transcontinental railroads in the nineteenth century to the arrival of the dispossessed from the dust bowl, though his personal viewpoint breaks through in such statements as, the migrants "are courageous, intelligent and resourceful."

In the rest of the article, set off from the introduction by double spacing, the writer's technique changes—"Let us see what the migrants from the dust bowl find when they arrive in California"—attempting to involve the reader in a shared discovery. A straightforward factual approach is sustained almost to the end of the third paragraph, when Steinbeck breaks loose with an emotionally charged personal statement, "It is often said that no one starves in the United States, yet in Santa Clara County last year five babies were certified by the local coroner to have died of malnutrition, the modern word for starvation."

From this point, two-thirds of the way through the article, all efforts at impersonality or impartiality disappear as the writer strives to carry readers with him through an increasingly charged denunciation of the conditions he has observed, culminating in the statement that "the large grower has changed anger into defensive fury." If the tone at the beginning is too distant to involve casual readers in the text, the transition to polemics may be too rapid. Steinbeck has not yet developed in journalism the pacing he had achieved in his fiction. This article is a somewhat fumbling beginning, but it remains important. This earliest treatment of the migrant problems shows the already clear commitment that would shape the making of Steinbeck's great novel.

"The Harvest Gypsies"

The series of seven articles Steinbeck wrote later under the collective title "The Harvest Gypsies" in September 1936 on commission for the *San Francisco News* covers the same ground as the *Nation* article, but in much more detail and from a consistent viewpoint. Steinbeck was beginning to feel more at home in a new medium and more self-confident about supplying information to a known audience in the hope of inspiring action. In view of the seriousness of the matters under discussion and despite occasional shrill outbursts from an overburdened sensibility, the tone of the articles is almost understated. Steinbeck is not lecturing but talking confidentially to readers he feels are well-intentioned, willing to look at some disturbing facts and to act in what is actually their own best interest. The journalistic impersonality of the *Nation* essay is maintained almost to the end of the later series, but the clipped style of the earlier introduction has been dropped, as is the traditional journalistic practice of providing all the principal information in the lead. The first day's report, "The People, Who They Are," which is about one-third again as long as the whole *Nation* article, is devoted to identifying the present migrants from the dust bowl. Their predecessors are mentioned only in passing until the final story in the series. Although the precise words are never used, the underlying question in the opening piece is, "You have seen these people, but do you know who they are?"

He does try to undermine any accusation of guilelessness in pleading the migrant's case by abruptly beginning the third paragraph, "In California we found a curious attitude toward a group that makes our agriculture successful. The migrants are needed, and they are hated."[3] This sardonic impugning of fellow Californians contrasts perhaps a little too much in tone with his idealistic generalizations about the migrants, which may have led to some uncertainty, particularly among Eastern intellectuals in the United States, about Steinbeck's disinterestedness in these reports and even in the novel to follow. Could he be taking up the migrants' cause to air a personal grudge against other native sons' neglect of his early fiction? He appears, however, from the tone of the columns to have been generally surprised and shocked by the violence of the reaction of many of his neighbors against his pleadings for compassion. He seems intent on making a case that he expects others to understand if they can only approach the matter thoughtfully. His picture of the migrants, however, as "men who have worked hard on their own farms and have felt the pride of possessing and living in close touch with the land" (French, 56), stakes his own case on the point, also lyrically made in *The Grapes of Wrath*, that there is some special virtue associated with living on and working one's own land. He goes on to stress that these migrant workers are wandering gypsies only because of circumstances beyond their control: "In their heads, as they move wearily from harvest to harvest, there is one urge and one overwhelming need, to acquire a little land again, and to settle on it and stop their wandering" (56). In contrast, he attacks the large growers on the grounds that they have made the migrants "strangely anachronistic" by developing "a system of agriculture so industrialized that the man who plants a crop does not often see, let alone harvest, the fruit of his planting" (57).

Underlying much of Steinbeck's work, as many critics beginning with Chester Eisinger have noticed, is an unshakable and perhaps irrational commitment to the concept of Thomas Jefferson's "independent yeoman" as the necessary cornerstone of a stable democratic society. Considering that Steinbeck concludes this opening essay with the threat that migrants will destroy "the present system of agricultural economics" if they continue to be handled "with the inhumanity and stupidity that have characterized the past" (59), one wonders what long-range solutions to the problems he may have envisioned. Most of his proposals in the following articles are only stopgaps.

Steinbeck's dramatic power of presenting a situation is demonstrated by the second article, "Squatters' Camps," the best-planned and most appealing of the group. He depicts the deterioration of the migrants' morale and lifestyle by contrasting three family groups: the first are newcomers to California, whose "spirit and sense of dignity have not quite been wiped out,"; the second are "middle-class" campers who have been on the road longer; and the third are in a terrible plight, exemplified by the father who has suffered a "loss of dignity and spirit" that has "cut him down to a kind of sub-humanity" (60–63). The first family, Steinbeck points out, will be in the position of the third within six months or a year.

He employs here a device that he will use with great success in *The Grapes of Wrath* and his pseudodocumentary film *The Forgotten Village*. He appeals to the readers' sympathies by presenting a problem involving masses of anonymous people through the portrayal of individual families with whom the kind of readers he sought could empathize.

He employs a countertechnique of depersonalizing the great landowners by associating them twice with the Fascists whose rise to power in Europe was just beginning to be seen as a threat in the United States. In the third article, "Corporation Farming," he describes he inadequacy of the housing they provide for the migrants. He depicts the growers as a powerful organized force seeking to keep innocent victims helpless by using both cooperative local law enforcement agencies and terrorist techniques to prevent the workers from organizing. The growers in the Imperial Valley had found a better way than costly anti-syndicalism trials to control the migrant workers on the growers' terms. According to Steinbeck, they had devised "a system of terrorism that would be unusual in the Fascist nations of the world" (69). He further claims that

"Fascistic methods are more numerous, more powerfully applied, and more openly practiced in California than any other place in the United States" (87). He would avoid such specific labels in *The Grapes of Wrath*, although it may have been such outbursts in "L'Affaire Lettuceberg" that caused him to destroy this novel and replace it with his great work.

A principal value of these articles today is the contrast they provide with *The Grapes of Wrath*, allowing us to contrast his first hurriedly expressed outrage at the appalling situations he had encountered with his carefully considered and artfully presented major work. They also refute objections that Steinbeck offered no solutions to the problems he presented. Even if his proposals would only have been stopgaps, the fourth article, "Government Housing," describes the camps at Arvin and Marysville, California, set up by the federal government for the migrants—the camps he used as models for the Weedpatch camp in *The Grapes of Wrath*.

In the fifth article, "Relief, Medicine, Income, Diet," he traces "the history of one family in relation to medicine, work relief, and direct relief" (75), indicating the migrants' inadequate diet and especially the problems at childbirth. The brief sixth article, "The Foreign Migrant," points out that "The history of California's importation and treatment of foreign labor is a disgraceful picture of greed and cruelty" (80), illustrating his charge with discussions of the virtual peonage into which Mexican, Chinese, Japanese, and Filipino immigrants were placed. He finally comments, however, that "Foreign labor is on the wane in California" (85)—a situation that has changed since World War II.

The seventh article, last of the original series, "The Future?" specifically lists the need for establishing a state migratory labor board on which workers would be represented and through which they could get accurate information about job possibilities as well as help for organizing to protect their rights. Such advocacy for solving these urgent problems through a humane and intelligent bureaucracy shows Steinbeck's differing conceptions in 1936 of the functions of journalism and fiction.

The newspaper stories argue with perhaps too much of the same truculence as the contending parties for what Thoreau would call "expedient" solutions rather than long-range planning. Steinbeck maintains, for example, at the conclusion of "The Harvest Gypsies" that the migrants "can be citizens of the highest type, or they can be an army driven by hatred and suffering to take what they need" (p. 87), which would devastatingly polarize the situation without getting at what Steinbeck called in a letter to a friend about his novel *In Dubious Battle* as "mere outcroppings." His claims for the migrants are not strengthened, however, by his example of one woman who has lost five children in six years before or just after birth because of malnutrition, but whose only self-criticism is of not having become pregnant during the other year.

In *The Grapes of Wrath*, however, his purpose is not to advocate mindless conformity to exhausted behavior patterns but to dramatize how through slow and painstaking self-education individuals have a capacity for change. His journalistic handling of the migrant problem in California is based on a phenomenological perception of the catastrophe that has disrupted the status quo and attempts to remedy it through properly respected democratic forums. The inefficiency of this approach is ironically demonstrated by his feeling obliged to observe in the spring of 1938, in an epilogue to "The Harvest Gypsies" stories for their publication as a pamphlet titled *Their Blood Is Strong*, that what was true two years ago in Nipomo is still true. He can report no progress but only reiterate the points he had already made. At this point, probably before he abandoned "L'Affaire Lettuceberg," he was still in the same apocalyptic mood in which he composed his earlier novels. "Must the hunger become anger and the anger fury before anything will be done?" (92), he must ask again.

The novel also ends, so far as the future of the Joad family as representative of the migrants is concerned, with a question about the future; but while it remains uncertain, he has created in the Joads individuals that prove capable of change, an example to be followed. Then what follows is left to the readers. One finishes the newspaper stories with no questions about the reporter's sincerity and integrity but with the feeling that he shares with some of the protagonists of his earlier fiction an outraged feeling that their effort has been wasted. In turning to *The Grapes of Wrath*, he would be moved by a different vision.

Working Days

We do not know what Steinbeck's thoughts or intentions were during the angry months that he spent churning out the finally suppressed "L'Affaire Lettuceberg," but half a century later readers were able to share his feelings and frustrations as he sped through his monumental work *The Grapes of Wrath*. In conjunction with the fiftieth anniversary of the publication of the novel, Steinbeck's estate in 1989 authorized the publication of a journal that he kept during the five months he worked on the manuscript from late in May until until 26 October 1938 at his homes in Los Gatos, California. (The Steinbecks moved during the course of the writing.)

There are few such diaries of the composition of a landmark work of fiction. Although Steinbeck refused to allow it to be published during his lifetime, he did consider the possibility of its being circulated some day, for he kept it a clear and readable work, not written in the kind of code or shorthand that some writers use for diaries. He had apparently forgotten about it, however, when he found it among his papers after his third marriage. He was tempted to destroy it, but sent it instead to Pascal Covici for safekeeping during his lifetime. His own handwritten copy has apparently been lost, but a stenographer at Viking Press transcribed it. If Steinbeck checked this copy, he made no corrections.

Robert DeMott, a distinguished Steinbeck scholar who had compiled a record of the author's library and reading, was selected to edit the typescript, along with some other dated entries, under the title *Working Days*.

It is certainly the most important autobiographical record that Steinbeck left. And it is very different from the journal he would keep thirteen years later. Then, living in a quite different style in a much changed world, he wrote a series of letters to his editor Pascal Covici, at the same time writing the other of his two longest and most demanding novels, *East of Eden*. (These letters have been published in *Journal of a Novel: The "East of Eden" Letters* [1969], discussed in chapter 8.) One of the most surprising features of *Working Days* is that it tells very little about the day-to-day development of the narrative but concentrates principally on the author's experience of physically writing it—his state of mind, the state of his health, his shifting feelings about what he was doing, his carefully planned writing schedule and the numerous obstacles to carrying it out.

Since the journal begins three days after he had started writing the novel in exactly what would be the order of the contents in the published book (except for a very few deletions and one short addition to an earlier chapter to explain the disappearance of the Joads' oldest son, Noah), there is no indication of just when he planned this narrative as a replacement for "L'Affaire Lettuceberg" or when he worked out the Joad story in detail and planned the placement of the interchapters. If he made a written outline of the chapter-by-chapter plan for the book, it has not been found. He does mention twice in the journal that he is not sure which of the interchapters (he calls them "general chapters") he will use at a given point; but he never mentions any alteration in his conception of the installments in the Joad story, as he does frequently in recounting his greater problems with the structuring of *East of Eden*.

Occasionally in *Working Days*, especially in early and very late entries, he mentions what material will be included in work planned for the next day, but one has to turn to the published text to understand them. (The diary entries were usually composed before resuming work on the novel each day, as a kind of limbering-up exercise.) One cannot follow the plot of the novel from the diary. What is most clearly accounted for there is the word-by-word progress of the book—how many pages were actually written each day.

He imposed a rigorous routine upon himself, though he did not attempt to establish an inflexible timetable for the project. His first entry specifies, "I have seven months to do this book and I should like to take them but I imagine five will be the limit" (20). He repeatedly bemoans falling behind schedule and, on the other hand, not allowing himself more time to relax; but he drove himself to finish in exactly five months, even though he usually worked only from Monday to Friday, using Saturdays for catch-ups if needed and leaving Sundays free, especially for numerous visitors. He could not hold rigorously to this schedule, for important visitors like Covici and Charlie Chaplin sometimes appeared during the week; and there were inescapable personal obligations. He was extraordinarily successful in maintaining a 2,000-word a day goal that produced 10,000 words a week.

Not surprisingly, Steinbeck's feelings toward the value and success of what he was doing fluctuated from day to day. Did he have any inkling that he might be writing what would become one of the most celebrated and controversial epic novels of the century? The first indication of his own ambitions and misgivings appears in the entry for 18 June (an unusual Saturday when he felt he needed to work a full day), as he moves into chapter 8 and its introduction to the whole Joad family, with whom he and the readers will make the long trek from the dust bowl to a dubious future in California: "If only I could do this book properly it would be one of the really fine books and a truly American book. But I am assailed with my own ignorance and inability" (29). He is driven, however, by a compulsion to get the book done, as well as by feelings that it may be the end of his career. On 19 October, as he nears the end of this long odyssey, misgivings overwhelm him: "I am sure of one thing—it isn't the great book I hoped it would be. It's just a run-of-the-mill book. And the awful thing is that it is absolutely the best that I can do" (90). How many such colossal misjudgments have other writers made? The next day he feels strong and achieves a psychic identification with Tom Joad, whose great speech to his mother Steinbeck had recently completed: "Funny where the energy comes from" (91). He greets the next week by saying, "I might as well get to the work. No one else is going to do it for me." On Wednesday, 26 October, he begins, "If I can finish today I won't care much what happens afterwards"; and he is able to append, "finished today—and I hope to God it's good" (93).

Chapter Three
Escape into the Sea of Cortez

Steinbeck's first published novel, *Cup of Gold*, was about an ambitious young Welshman who escapes an unpromising home and goes to sea as a pirate to end up as a colonial governor. Steinbeck's first published non-fiction book is about an idealistic young man who also seeks to escape a deteriorating situation at home and goes to sea with ambitions to become a marine biologist, but his voyage lasts only a few weeks before he returns home to vacillate between two careers. This man is Steinbeck himself; the book is *Sea of Cortez;* and, although he was already an internationally renowned, best-selling author, his new book portended little brighter future for its author than that first novel.

Steinbeck had not expected *The Grapes of Wrath* to be such a phenomenal and disastrous success. Only two days before finishing the novel, he expressed uneasiness about Pascal Covici's "volatile" liking for the book, "I hope he doesn't oversell it. Too many superlatives can spoil its chances" (*Working Days*, 91). Robert DeMott quotes him as warning his agents not to let Covici push the book too hard, but Viking Press went ahead with an aggressive campaign, which proved hardly necessary as the novel's reputation spread by word of mouth from enthusiastic or outraged readers (170). As Steinbeck wrote a year later, on 16 October 1939, after he had been suffering for months with a leg infection, "*The Grapes of Wrath* really got out of hand, became a public hysteria, and I became a public domain" (105). He feels he must be "born again," but he feels that his new sources must be found "in the tide pool and on a microscope slide rather than in men" (*Working Days*, 106).

This attempted rebirth was to have manifested itself in two related projects that he had been contemplating since he had been working on *The Grapes of Wrath*. At that time his friend Ed Ricketts had been working with another writer, Jack Calvin, on a study of the marine life of the Pacific Coast. Their book, *Between Pacific Tides*, was published by Stanford University Press the same month of April 1939 as *The Grapes of Wrath*. When the editor of the press proposed that Ricketts might follow it up with a pamphlet for school use, Steinbeck was attracted by the idea of collaborating with Ricketts on a study of the littoral of the San Francisco

Bay area, from which could be developed a high school textbook that would establish Steinbeck's credentials as a scientific writer. Meanwhile, Steinbeck could lend the venture the prestige of his name and the benefit of his style in converting Ricketts's notes into attractive prose. Then would follow a joint expedition into the Gulf of California—also known as the Sea of Cortez—which would lead to a significant contribution to the scientific knowledge of the area. Presumably subsequent joint ventures would provide a detailed account of the Pacific littoral.

Steinbeck plunged enthusiastically into this task during the autumn and winter of 1939–40, writing a preface and about 3,000 words for the essay section of a proposed 200–250 page book. He began to find, however, that the demand for scientific accuracy left him little room for imagination or individuality. The work became difficult and uncongenial, and nothing finally came of the project despite some collecting expeditions that he and Ricketts made. They resolved to go ahead with the more ambitious expedition anyway. Originally, they had intended to make it by truck into the sparsely populated and generally inhospitable lands of Mexico's Baja California peninsula, but as soon as they began to plan the trip (which Steinbeck would finance with profits from his novel), they realized that they could not survey the shore of the gulf from the peninsula's primitive roads but would have to charter a boat. Determining that one of the purse seiners used to catch sardines for the then-thriving Monterey canneries would be ideal for hiring during off-season at the plants, they finally settled on the *Western Flyer*.[1] They left Monterey on 11 March, returning on 13 April.

The book was to be a collaboration, composed on the lines of the now-abandoned handbook. Both men would keep logs during the journey, and Steinbeck would then work with these and any other relevant materials to amalgamate the separate contributions. As it turned out, Steinbeck did not keep a log, so that Ricketts provided the necessary data. Steinbeck combined this with materials provided by the captain of the boat and three crewmen, as well as his own recollections and speculations. His wife Carol was also on the trip, but she apparently did not contribute to the book, and her presence provided some problems both during the trip and in the construction of the narrative.

With the trip over, Steinbeck settled down in Monterey to fabricate a "log" for the expedition, even though the publisher had not been decided upon. The most frequently used source of Steinbeck's text to the *Sea of Cortez*—and the one cited here—was published in 1951 as *The Log from "Sea of Cortez."* Pascal Covici wanted Viking to publish it as a follow-up to *The Grapes of Wrath*, capitalizing on the novel's reputation (it remained a best-seller for two years). The collaborators wanted it to be published by Stanford University Press as a companion to Ricketts's book with Jack Calvin. The press would want to emphasize the findings of the expedition, while Viking would look for an emphasis on travels in an exotic and little-known region by a celebrity author about whom the public sought information. Viking finally became the publisher after Covici promised to produce a large-format book, elegantly printed, with color-plate reproductions of the catalogued specimens.

Sales were disappointing. The high-priced book was designed to catch the eye of the Christmas shoppers, but the attack on Pearl Harbor in 1941 dampened holiday spirits. In addition, the packaging and promotion of the book may have been viewed with suspicion by the scientific community that Steinbeck and Ricketts hoped to reach. Copies of the original edition are now few and command high prices in the collectors' market.

As the abandonment of the proposed textbook indicates, Steinbeck was frustrated by the technical exactness and professional impersonality scientific writing demanded. His mind was not primarily on "the tide-pools" but on "the stars." He got restless with his self-imposed task even before he was finished. While there is a leisurely and entertaining account of the preparations for the expedition, there is almost nothing about the return trip. The account cuts off summarily as the *Western Flyer* rounds Cap San Lucas and heads back up the Pacific. The most important thing that Steinbeck's log makes clear is that his future did not lie with the "tidepools and microscopes." *Sea of Cortez* is another false start toward a career in a new field of writing.

Steinbeck's Log as Autobiography

As Pascal Covici, who was delighted with the tone of the early chapters, had guessed, a main source of interest in the book was its revelation (albeit limited) of Steinbeck's personal interests. Covici did not even wish to acknowledge Ricketts as a collaborator. Previously Steinbeck had been elusive and evasive, shunning public appearances and interviews, but the public wanted information about the author of *The Grapes of Wrath* and *Of Mice and Men*, his two most recent and extraordinarily successful and controversial novels. He did not reveal much in *Sea of Cortez*, but it is the first book in which what he had to say about himself was more interesting than the work at hand. One difficulty in following the travelogue as a personal diary is that Steinbeck, to stress the collaborative nature of the work, steadily uses "we" instead of "I" to describe his and Ricketts's activities. The result is that the reader can't get an individualized sense of the two men. The persistent use of the first-person plural also necessitates awkward shifts in sentence structure when Steinbeck attributes some past action to an unspecified member of the expedition.

Confusion is further compounded by Steinbeck's failure to mention that his first wife, Carol, is one of the party. He refers to seven people being aboard the *Western Flyer* but identifies only six. This omission is often attributed to the deterioration of the couple's relationship that would lead to their separation not long afterward. Steinbeck might have been reluctant to talk about her, and she might not have wanted to be mentioned. Another explanation is that Steinbeck was putting together most of "The Log" while he was hiding out with Gwyn Conger, who would become his second wife, and he may not have wanted her to see references to Carol. There may, however, be another even more quirksome explanation to account for this curious feature. Toward the end of the narrative, Steinbeck mentions the existence of a strong prejudice against women in scientific accounts of marine expeditions. If a woman is on a ship, "she is never called by her name or referred to as an equal. In the account she emerges as 'the shipmate,' 'the skipper,' 'the pal.' She is nearly always a stringy blonde with leathery skin who is included in all photographs to give them 'interest.'"[2] Steinbeck thus may simply have been following custom, seeking, as a newcomer to such ventures, to establish his credentials for membership in a professional circle. But he goes on to say that "this stringy shipmate" is "slightly obscene to use," making one wonder why he adopted a practice that he appears to disdain.

His comment about the "equality" of all members of the party also directs attention to the portrayal of the four hired members of the crew—including the owner of the boat—who are not included in the collective "we," even if Carol is supposed to have been, since she participated in most of the actual collecting of specimens. Tony, the master, is treated throughout the narrative with a kind of distancing dignity. His concern for his own appearance and that of the ship, for the safety of the vessel, and for strict adherence to his orders about the ship's course is stressed. Steinbeck's references to Tony are generally limited to his command function, and relations between the employer and the commander seem to have been somewhat strained. Steinbeck's treatment of the three crewmen, on the other hand, is somewhat like his treatment of the paisanos in *Tortilla Flat* and "the boys" in *Cannery Row*, affectionate but somewhat condescending. According to Sparky Enea's later account of the trip, Steinbeck's relations with the crewmen were quite friendly and informal, but they had some problems getting along with Carol.[3]

Steinbeck's principal interest in introducing this first public recounting of an important episode in his life was to experiment in a new genre. "The design of a book," he writes, "is the pattern of a reality controlled and shaped by the mind of the author. This is completely understood about poetry or fiction, but it is too seldom realized about books of fact" (*Log*, 1). He goes on to talk about the "shape" of the trip, but what this means never becomes clear to the reader. He simply recounts on a day-by-day basis the visiting of predetermined ports of call to collect specimens. Indeed, he comments that he could have done several different things—unspecified—about the design, but "we have decided to let it form itself." The "design" of a narrative conventionally depends on elements of surprise or suspense, the introduction of new characters or situations; but there are few of these in this account of the collecting expedition, except when Steinbeck from time to time interrupts the diary of the trip with some metaphysical speculations. The effectiveness of a book about travels depends largely on the traveler's impression of the places he visits and the people he meets or travels with. Steinbeck had up to this time been a reclusive person who shunned publicity, and he was probably still uneasy about revealing too much of himself and his relationships with others. The sparsely populated desert-like region that was the subject of the expedition offered few varieties of experience, and the collecting work soon become repetitive. The plan for this junket provided few opportunities for exotic or thrilling experiences, and Steinbeck had not set out in quest of adventure.

Steinbeck, however, was not content to allow his after-the-fact log to become merely a scientific notebook or a how-to guide for a project that few others would likely undertake. The real "design" behind the book that Steinbeck disingenuously chooses not to stress was not only to establish his credentials as a scientific researcher but also to get into print some of his friend Ed Ricketts's metaphysical speculations, which Ricketts had not been able to place in the learned journals where such material usually appears. Perhaps the most controversial aspect of this publication was the attribution of authorship. Pascal Covici wished to assign the log to Steinbeck alone and give Ricketts credit for only the illustrated catalogue of specimens that accompanied the original edition, but Steinbeck insisted that Ricketts be given full credit as coauthor.

The concern of this book is primarily with Steinbeck's nonfiction writings as fragments of an autobiography. As such, it is not an appropriate place to enter into or summarize the long, complicated, and sometimes acidulous discussion among literary specialists about who is responsible for some of the ideas advanced in the log—Steinbeck or Ricketts—that has flourished since the publication of Richard Astro's *John Steinbeck and Edward F. Ricketts: The Shaping of a Novelist* in 1973.[4] I support Roy Simmonds's position that Steinbeck is responsible for the style and contents of the log and that what amounts to an interpolated essay or non-teleological thinking (chapter 14) must be judged on its own merits and cannot usefully be challenged on the basis of opinions expressed in his other publications.

Such a disclaimer must be accompanied, however, by an admission that *Sea of Cortez* is of limited value as an autobiographical work. Steinbeck observes in his introduction that the subject of the book is "everything we could see and think and even imagine" (*Log*, 1). There was little variety, however, in what was to be seen; and very little is actually said about what happened during the interactions between four seamen, two friends, and the disaffected wife of one of them during a month spent in close quarters on a small vessel, with few visits to shore to meet other people. Those interested in getting the lowdown will find their curiosity better rewarded by *With Steinbeck in the Sea of Cortez* (1991), an account of the trip as told to Audry Lynch by Sparky Enea, who was the radioman on the *Western Flyer* during the expedition.

The Log as Metaphysical Speculation

If Steinbeck does not go much beyond the difficulties of collecting specimens of life on the littoral, he does fulfill his promise to dig deeply into what was thought—or perhaps the more accurate word is *imagined*—by him and Ricketts during the hours devoted to metaphysical speculation rather than personal relations.

One problem of "shaping" the text that Steinbeck encountered was that of how to introduce material that did not develop naturally out of the course of events. He evidently had some qualms about digressing into such matters when he chose a lazy Easter Sunday, when the party was not collecting "strongly or very efficiently," to shift, quite peremptorily, to a discussion of "manners of thinking and matters of thinking," which he immediately admits defensively "is not stylish any more" (*Log*, 131). Steinbeck is beginning to feel at odds with much of the culture in which he had grown up.

The matter toward which he has been edging is "non-teleological thinking," which he defines as " 'is' thinking that might be substituted in part for the usual cause-effect methods" (*Log*, 132). Such thinking concerns itself, he goes on, "primarily not with what should be, or could be, or might be, but rather with what actually 'is'—attempting at most to answer the already sufficiently difficult questions *what* or *how*, instead of *why*" (*Log*, 135).

Actually, this expedition on the *Western Flyer* could itself be offered as an outcome of non-teleological thinking, for it was limited to questions of *what*, *where*, and *when*, with the *how* provided by bringing together a researcher qualified to direct the collecting, someone with the money to pay the bills, and someone willing to provide the boat. Still, inevitably, the question of *why* arises. Granting the presence of these particular components, why should they come together in this fashion? The problem seems hardly metaphysical—everyone involved got something that he wanted. Tony made some money during an off-season; Ricketts, who had had trouble getting published, saw some of his ideas finally in print; and Steinbeck got his way about the credits for the log. Where is the problem of understanding? Actually the problem is that teleology has not really been explained in the log because of an ambiguity in the meaning of the key word *why*.

Non-teleological thinking, Steinbeck explains, considers "events as outgrowths and expressions rather than as results" (*Log*, 135): but "outgrowths and expressions" are forms of results. Their distinction is that they are not *predestined* results. Teleological thinking is based on the conception that everything that happens has been prearranged by some supernatural force. It is the basis of all forms of fortune-telling—if one can just break the code, one can control the universe. Non-teleological thinking is based on the conception that something can be explained only after it has happened—if then. The problem with *Sea of Cortez* as metaphysical speculation is not that such practice is no longer stylish but that this book—this most often cited and argued example of it—is not a very helpful aid in understanding it.

Steinbeck also seems to have become tired of writing the book. He frequently complains in letters to Pascal Covici about having trouble with it; and, after the *Western Flyer* is reported to have left the gulf and turned northward in the Pacific Ocean on 13 April, there are only five concluding paragraphs to sum up the expedition. There are no final speculations about what the expedition accomplished. Steinbeck makes a stab at supplying some by observing, "The shape of the trip was an integrated nucleus from which weak strings of thought stretched out into every reachable reality, and a reality which reached into us through our perceptive nerve trunks" (*Log*, 270). But what does this mean in communicable terms? A more satisfactory ending is provided then by the simple statement, "We liked it very much." It was a happy escape, but Steinbeck remains vague about just what he—or "we"—liked about it. As a model for vacation planning, its applications appear limited.

To make a final, non-teleological judgment, requiring that one approach a task with no preconceived expectations, the *is* material in the log—the *what* and *how* of the expedition—do not reveal much about the author, while the speculative material unintentionally does. But the report may provide a small reward for the reader's investment in it. As the first ambitious move toward an alternative career, this book reveals primarily that Steinbeck was not yet able or willing to exploit his own personality as marketable merchandise.

The Log Revived as a Tribute to Ed Ricketts

In 1951, when Steinbeck's reputation needed some boosting, as Viking Press, his publisher, eagerly awaited his second big novel, *East of Eden*, it was decided to reprint the ten-year-old *Log from "Sea of Cortez"* as a separate title. It would be published without the color plates in the original but with a new introductory essay by Steinbeck, "About Ed Ricketts," as a tribute to his friend who had been killed in 1948 in an automobile-train collision in Monterey.

This sixty-page memoir was a new kind of writing for Steinbeck, but he had learned a lot about writing about actual rather than fictional events from his newspaper dispatches. From his experience with the original log, he may have learned that assuming that if the writer told the truth the facts would find their own form did not always produce satisfactory results. The Ricketts essay is a noteworthy companion to the log, because whereas the earlier work was quite artless for an experienced writer, the memorial essay proves almost too artfully contrived to suit its purpose. Steinbeck had not yet found the middle ground required by the provocative kind of nonfiction he sought to write, in which the writer confides enough about himself to establish his authority without becoming overbearingly authoritative.

The publishers had expected a factual profile of Ricketts, emphasizing his qualifications as a marine biologist, and they were somewhat distressed at receiving a rambling collection of impressionistic reminiscences. Steinbeck wrote to a friend who had known both him and Ricketts during the 1930s that he thought his account would be "much more effective with people who did not know" Ricketts, since Steinbeck "was trying to put down a feeling and an effect rather than a factual matter" (Benson, 671). What he was trying to do was not to let people make up their own minds about Ricketts but to try to make them feel the way that Steinbeck felt about him. This effort was particularly significant in contemplating similarities and differences between ostensibly factual and fictional materials, because in the course of the essay Steinbeck attributes many of the characteristics and behavior of Doc in the novel *Cannery Row* to Ricketts. Many people were not surprised by these revelations, of course, but Steinbeck's design here offers unusual evidence of the way in which material used to produce enjoyable fiction may also be used to try to evoke warm feelings for an actual person.

Steinbeck's technique in the article in many ways resembles that of J. D. Salinger in his crowning effort on the fictional Glass family, the story "Seymour: An Introduction," (1959). Salinger has his alter ego, Buddy Glass, describe his older brother Seymour, now deceased, as "our consultant genius, our portable conscience," whose "character lends itself to no legitimate sort of narrative compactness that *I* know of."[5] Steinbeck could have said the same thing about Ricketts. He often borrows precise phrases from *Cannery Row* to describe Ricketts in the essay; perhaps one of the most cited examples is "His mind had no horizon."[6] Even Steinbeck's discussion of the technique he uses in the memoir echoes *Cannery Row*. He says of Ricketts: "He was so complex and many-faceted that perhaps the best method will be to go from one facet of him to another so that from all the bits a whole picture may build itself for me as well as for others" (*The Log*, xxxix). This closely resembles his description of what is the best way to write his novel *Cannery Row*: "to open the page and let the stories crawl in by themselves" (ix). This, in turn, resembles Buddy Glass's conception of himself trying to describe brother Seymour: "What I am, I think, is a thesaurus of undetached prefatory remarks about him. . . . I don't dare go anywhere near the short-story form" (Salinger, 125). Both Salinger and Steinbeck are attempting *not* to tell readers what they think about their characters but to share with them impressions that they hope will make readers see the characters that way for themselves.

It probably should not be surprising, therefore, that the novel conveys a more vivid impression of Ricketts than the memoir. When Steinbeck is discussing his real friend in the memoir, he hesitates to broach the touchy issue of Ricketts's sex life; in the novel he can write with startling brevity, "He was concupiscent as a rabbit and gentle as hell" (*Cannery Row*, 23). Troublesome realities that might distract one from the image in the memoir, like wife and children, can be dispensed with in the novel.

The memorialist also has to respect some conventions that do not influence the novelist, so that the invitational tone of "About Ed Ricketts" becomes sometimes heavy-handed as Steinbeck must find some way to wind up his long eulogy: "I have tried to isolate and inspect the great talent that was in Ed Ricketts, that made him so loved and needed and makes him so missed now that he is dead" (*The Log*, lxiv). Nothing like this need intervene between the reader and the character in a novel, and if it should (as sometimes in Salinger's stories), accusations of preaching are likely to follow. The novelist can disappear into his text. Steinbeck, for example, preferred to make Tom Joad into an inspirational background voice in *The Grapes of Wrath*. His problem as reporter and memorialist was to develop a position where he could feel comfortable between the text and the reader.

An explanation of the process of self-discovery that Steinbeck attributes to Ricketts in *The Log* may well describe a phase of his own coming out of seclusion to hold a lantern up for the world. Ricketts explained to Steinbeck that, for a long time, "I did not like myself for a number of reasons, some of them valid and some of them pure fancy. . . . Then gradually . . . I discovered with surprise and pleasure that people did like me. And I thought, if they can like me, why cannot I like myself? Just thinking did not do it, but slowly I learned to like myself and then it was all right" (*The Log*, lxv). Steinbeck never made such a complete adjustment, but he learned that "Once Ed was able to like himself he was released from the secret prison of self-contempt" (*The Log*, lxvi); and he provided Steinbeck with a key to his own release. Steinbeck did owe Ricketts a great deal; but in this essay he begins to find ways to share this legacy with others.

The unfortunate decision that may some day yet be rectified was to use this memorial tribute as a preface to *The Log from "Sea of Cortez"* rather than as an epilogue to a new edition of *Cannery Row*, where it would certainly have been likely to reach many more readers and to serve as an immediate guide to the realities behind the fiction.

Chapter Four

Artist as Propagandist

Between John Steinbeck's compilation of the log for *Sea of Cortez* and his ransacking of his memories of happier days for "About Ed Ricketts," he had learned a new trade that greatly influenced his ability to come out from behind his writings and deal directly with the public with greater self-confidence. He became a propagandist. There were propagandistic aspects, of course, to his writings about migrant workers in California, but he was careful to campaign for expedient action, preferring that responsible people make the difficult choice of educating themselves. He tried to make people think for themselves rather than telling them exactly what he thought they should think. In educational jargon, one might say that he sought to motivate readers rather than indoctrinate them. Until the unexpected success of *The Grapes of Wrath* and the agonizing collapse of his first marriage in 1940, Steinbeck shunned the spotlight and, though he never put the practice so bluntly himself, held to the doctrine that while he could support changes that might better human conditions, someone else was going to have to take the initiative in publicizing them.

Through this period Steinbeck continued to manifest the qualities of one who moves ahead of the frontier. He was not only a Westerner but one of an old breed harking back to James Fenimore Cooper's Leatherstocking. Among the memorable characters that Steinbeck created, the one he most resembled was Jody Tiflin's frustrated grandfather in "The Leader of the People," the story that closes *The Red Pony* cycle. Like him, Steinbeck restlessly sought new worlds to conquer and lamented the loss of the spirit of "Westering"—pushing beyond new frontiers—in later generations. In the popular media of the 1930s these characteristics were embodied in the Lone Ranger, that masked man on the white horse who lived beyond the edge of civilization and yet, when duty called, galloped into corrupt situations, set them aright, and—shouting "Hi-yo, Silver"—took off for the next battleground. Although, there are some striking parallels between the popular program and Steinbeck's fiction, it is hard to imagine John Steinbeck listening to radio's Lone Ranger. The show went on the air in 1933, the same year that Steinbeck published "The Gift," the opening story of *The Red Pony* cycle, about Jody Tiflin, who yearns to be a leader of the people, like his grandfather. The challenge of new frontiers still had a strong hold on the American imagination. The show was the top thriller with a western setting in 1940, the year *The Grapes of Wrath* was still at the of top of best-seller lists. The Lone Ranger moved to television in 1949 and was one of the ten most popular shows in 1950, when Steinbeck was struggling to create his own man on a white horse from the Mexican revolutionary leader Emiliano Zapata and, less successfuly, to communicate the message that "every man is father to all children," through his complex symbolic drama *Burning Bright*. The Lone Ranger rides through many of Steinbeck's fables. (Steinbeck also had much in common with Richard Halliburton [1900–39?], a popular explorer/writer who disappeared during one of his expeditions.)

Immediately after winning the Pulitzer Prize for *The Grapes of Wrath*, however, in the spring of 1940, before the log from the *Sea of Cortez* expedition had been readied for publication, Steinbeck went back to Mexico to participate in the making of a short narrative film, *The Forgotten Village*, about the need for acceptance of modern medicine in superstitious rural areas still dominated by traditional witch doctors. Steinbeck chose to work with Herbert Kline, a European documentarian whose *Lights Out in Europe*, about the rise of fascism, had been widely acclaimed. Kline wanted to make a film about a Mexican peasant family's involvement in a revolutionary movement.

Steinbeck insisted on combining Kline's idea with that of the introduction of modern medicine to poor rural areas, thus making a film about a peaceful revolution mounted to save lives. The film is usually described as a documentary, but it isn't; it is not a record of actual events but rather a fictional narrative written by Steinbeck to advance what he thought a worthy cause—a technique he would soon be using again. It was filmed in Mexico with a nonprofessional native cast, so that it would look authentic, but it is actually a pseudodocumentary, a form that employs "location shooting" with ordinary people of the area to provide a backdrop for the author's superimposed message.

The nature of the film bears mention here because it is Steinbeck's first venture in a form that is nearly as old as commercial cinema—the British used it to win support for the Boer Wars at the end of the nineteenth century, and it has been frequently used since, as Steinbeck used it, both to promote charitable causes and to win patriotic support in wartime. This is not the occasion for a detailed investigation of the history of the pseudodocumentary as a means of promoting causes for both the better and the worse; but the difference between the true documentary and the pseudodocumentary—something not always ascertainable—may be suggested by the difference between two famous films Leni Riefenstahl made in the 1930s for Adolf Hitler.

Although both much studied films were heavily influenced by the techniques of German expressionism in distorting their materials, *The Triumph of the Will*, filmed in 1935 during the Nazi Party rally in Nuremberg, is a glorified newsreel, whereas *Olympia*, filmed during the 1936 Olympic Games, is a fantasy, communicating a personal artistic vision. The former was just what the Nazis wanted; the latter, what Riefenstahl wanted. *Triumph of the Will* features protracted shots of masses of men and women marching, saluting Der Führer, carrying banners blazoned with swastikas; human beings are reduced to automata, zombies, as they appear to carry out a ritual that merges them into one mass identity. Although Hitler had supposedly granted Riefenstahl complete artistic freedom, she had to operate under constraints that kept the political motivations behind the film always foremost. It is a document that was made to reinforce an ideology, not to send a new message. Riefenstahl was given a much freer hand with *Olympia*. She did not want to make "just a newsreel film." Renata Berg-Pan argues that the director realized that "the film would only be interesting if she could catch the form (*Gestaltung*) of the events, by which she means the collective image, not names and statistics, not records and figures."[1]

Especially in the famous diving scenes, Riefenstahl abandons any effort just to record the performances of the athletes and instead enters into a glorification of the human body. In this film, the Olympic Games become not an end in themselves but a means of capturing a personal artistic vision—the same aim that has driven many twentieth-century painters. In a much more modest way, Steinbeck aimed at the same goal in *The Forgotten Village*. He used ordinary people in their accustomed setting to create not a damning indictment of a backward culture, like that in Luis Buñuel's *Las Hurdes (Land without Bread)*, but a vision of possibilities that might make people arise to realize their potential.

From Personal to National Politics

An unexpected upshot of Steinbeck's trip to Mexico is a letter he wrote on 24 June 1940, in which he moves even more ambitiously from his former stance as "outsider" to that of "insider," seeking a direct hand in the shaping of the future. On a visit to Washington, D.C., after returning from Mexico, he wrote directly to President Roosevelt, probably encouraged to make what might be considered a presumptuous gesture by some approbatory remarks by Mrs. Roosevelt about *The Grapes of Wrath*. (She would later help Steinbeck get the New York State Board of Censors to lift a ban that had been placed on *The Forgotten Village* because it showed a childbirth.) To the president, Steinbeck wrote that his experiences while making "a little moving picture in Mexico" had led him to believe that "a crisis in the Western Hemisphere is imminent" and that he should be glad to speak to the president if his observations could be of any value (*Letters*, 206).

Poet Archibald MacLeish, then librarian of Congress, recommended a meeting, at which Steinbeck urged Roosevelt to set up a propaganda office that would use radio and motion pictures "to get this side of the world together." The president took no immediate action, but in September 1941 Steinbeck was summoned to Washington for a conference with "Wild Bill" Donovan, a Republican from New York who, after making suggestions similar to Steinbeck's, was appointed as head of the Office of Strategic Services. The new agency was to include a Foreign Information Service, headed by prominent playwright and later Roosevelt biographer Robert E. Sherwood, who called the meeting at which Steinbeck met with Thornton Wilder, Stephen Vincent Benét, and prominent journalists (Benson, 487). Benson reports that Steinbeck was offered a job with the office of the Coordinator of Information (COI) but turned it down, although he subsequently worked for it, probably without pay. It is for this agency, which later became the CIA, that he wrote his novel *The Moon Is Down*.

This work generated considerable controversy as novel, play, and movie. Its only relation to Steinbeck's nonfiction is that he wrote it as a propaganda piece. Still, it was an entirely fictitious tale, arguing that continued underground resistance in occupied countries would eventually wear down a conquering force (presumably, the Nazis) that had been mobilized by hypnotic propaganda (like Riefenstahl's). The work was criticized in the United States as not vilifying the occupying power strongly enough. Steinbeck stressed that in using a pseduodocumentary literary method (as in *Bombs Away*, 1942, discussed below), he was not trying to portray the German invaders but was seeking to universalize his message. The novel was greatly admired in the occupied countries, where resistance groups risked their lives to distribute it.[2] After the war, Steinbeck was awarded the Norway Cross by King Haakon for the film.

Steinbeck evidently did a great deal more work for the COI and other government agencies to promote the war effort, much of it ephemeral morale-building "crap," as he put it, that somebody had to produce. The novels that are surely the longest two of these patriotic efforts deserve mention because of their disillusioning effects on both Steinbeck and his fans. Neither, however, really belongs in an account of the development of his alternative career as a nonfiction writer; but both indicate problems that he encountered as a propagandist.

Much of Steinbeck's wartime work did not improve his professional reputation. In May 1942, he was asked by the government to write a book about the training of a bomber team. He did not care for the idea and tried to beg off, but finally consented after what amounted to a direct order in affectionate patriotic terms by President Roosevelt.

The result, *Bombs Away*, is one of the weakest, least impressive of his books to be published by his regular commercial house, Viking Press. It is usually viewed without much critical scrutiny as a straightforward report on the training of a bombing team, but it isn't. Like *The Forgotten Village*, it is a pseudodocumentary that, like Leni Riefenstahl's *Olympia*, is not concerned with "names and statistics" but the creation of a "collective image." It narrates not the training of one particular bomber crew among many but the training of an idealized crew—a military version of the Olympic diving team, but this time the author's heart wasn't in it. The book lacks the dynamic, individualistic drive of the Mexican film, the hypnotic aestheticism of *Olympia*, in which individuals are subordinated to a classic vision of ideal form, or even the optimistic vision of *The Moon Is Down*. Stylistically—as may have been best suited to its potential consumers—*Bombs Away* is closer to a comic book, probably the most popular form of American literature at that time. (Steinbeck was enthusiastic about at least some comic books; he wrote an introduction to Al Capp's *The World of L'il Abner* [1953].)

Another venture that pays tribute to our men who won the war led to another disaster—involving a much better work than *Bombs Away*—that was so far removed from Steinbeck's intentions when it finally reached the public that he petitioned unsuccessfully to have his name removed from the credits. In January 1943, Twentieth Century–Fox, which had filmed *The Grapes of Wrath* and *The Moon Is Down*, asked Steinbeck to write a script for an Alfred Hitchcock film that had been requested by the Maritime Commission as a tribute to the merchant seamen who risked their lives in waters infested with German U-boats.

Steinbeck was enthusiastic about this project and resurrected a manuscript that he had begun in 1941 about the victims of a U-boat sinking as a microcosmic world adrift (Benson, 511). Again he envisioned using a pseudodocumentary technique, employing allegorical characters to make the ordeal as realistic as possible. He prepared a story treatment called *Lifeboat* in the form of a novelette, from which he would create and deliver a script. The writing of the script, however, was assigned to others. Neither Steinbeck nor his estate has allowed his story treatment to be published, because he disowned the entire venture after he found that Hitchcock and Darryl Zanuck had completely distorted his intentions. He asked to have his name removed from the screen credits, but it was not, in a striking example of how commercial interests, in seeking to exploit the reputation of a distinguished and patriotic American, can damage it by imposing their political agenda on his story. Steinbeck obtained some revenge for this affront by describing the famous director of suspense films as "one of those English middle class snobs who really and truly despise working people" (*Life in Letters*, 267).

His most important work as a propagandist during the war, however, was kept totally secret at the time and throughout Steinbeck's lifetime. We know of it now through the research of a dedicated scholar, Cliff Lewis, who explains in this concise statement Steinbeck's contribution to Franklin D. Roosevelt's unprecedented and bitterly contested campaign for a fourth term in 1944.

> What "useful writing" had Steinbeck done for the campaign? First, he drafted a document in the form of a "letter" that FDR's staff drew upon for a campaign *Letter* sent to the Democratic Party Chairman [Senator Robert E. Hannegan] that was published July 11, 1944. Second, Steinbeck drafted another campaign document, a list of eleven principles, which he titled "Manefesto [*sic*]." These principles are the basis for FDR's presidential goals delivered to the Democratic National Convention as an acceptance speech titled *Address* on July 20, 1944. And they became the policies of the Truman administration.[3]

Lewis goes on to compare Steinbeck's draft proposals with the *Letter* and *Address* as delivered. Both toned down Steinbeck's bold assertions somewhat. Lewis comments in a later article, which also tells much more about Steinbeck's partisan writings during the period, that "Roosevelt and his speechwriters absorbed only part of the poetry into their dreary prose."[4]

Apparently, no further contributions were asked of Steinbeck during the campaign, but these stirring pieces obviously promoted his reputation in a new role with Democratic Party leaders. Late in his life, in one of his "Letters to Alicia" (11 December 1965), Steinbeck states that although relatively few people were aware of his service, he was an adviser to President Truman as well as to Roosevelt, Kennedy, and Johnson.

Nothing has so far been published about his relations with Harry Truman.

His association with and admiration of Adlai Stevenson are well known. He not only provided ideas for Stevenson's campaign but, in his most conspicuous display of partisanship to that point, contributed a foreword to a collection of Stevenson's speeches published during the 1952 presidential campaign. There Steinbeck states that he had been solidly behind Eisenhower (as Truman had been when he tried to convince the general to run on the Democratic ticket), but that he had been won over to Stevenson by his speeches. He praises Stevenson for touching on "no political, economic, or moral subject on which he has not taken a clear and open stand." In contrast was Eisenhower's seeming inability "to take any kind of stand on any subject." He observes that he cannot recall any speeches other than Stevenson's that "have made people unsatisfied with a digest. We want the thing in the man's own words."[5] Lewis reports that in 1956 Steinbeck also wrote a brief nominating speech for Estes Kefauver, who became Stevenson's vice-presidential running mate.

Little of this important material about Steinbeck's politicization has been discussed by his biographers, and more research needs to be done to understand his increasing involvement in partisan politics, which accounted for his relationship with President Lyndon B. Johnson and resulted in his alienation from much of the American literary community. Certainly this lone ranger finally dropped his mask and exposed himself to some bitter criticism as a propagandist. Steinbeck was not, however, misled into taking this role late in his life, as is often supposed because of his close and open association with President Lyndon B. Johnson. He had been operating behind the scenes since the success of *The Grapes of Wrath,* and despite the problems it caused him, this made him feel that he was not a prophet without honor but a voice that commanded respect in high places.

Chapter Five
Once There Was a War

In the spring of 1943, Steinbeck received permission to visit the Mediterranean theater of operations and send back dispatches to the New York *Herald Tribune*. These dispatches contain some of his most effective nonfiction writing, but they have never become really well known, even to devoted readers of his fiction. The major reason is that for fifteen years most of them lay buried in old files of the syndicate of newspapers that had published eighty-five of them between 21 June and 10 December 1943. (Five, including two about a Private Big Train Mulligan, whom Steinbeck had met, were included in the enlarged edition of *The Portable Steinbeck*, edited by Pascal Covici in 1946.)

By the time in 1958 that Covici decided to resurrect them under a collective title, *Once There Was a War* (nineteen were omitted), with a new introduction by Steinbeck, accounts of World War II aroused little interest. The United States was already becoming involved in new conflicts in Southeast Asia, turning itself into a kind of world police force.

Saber rattling was becoming unpopular. Following the vindication of Allen Ginsberg's hysterically anti-establishment poem *Howl* at a censorship trial in 1957 at the same time that Jack Kerouac's underground novel, *On the Road*, was greeted by a thriving market, the peacenik Beats were as much emulated by a restless young generation as they were denounced by their uptight elders. The older generation disapproved the policy of disengagement advocated by their sons and daughters, just as the powers that be trounced Steinbeck for his advocacy of social responsibility two decades earlier.

Steinbeck had not enjoyed much success since the mixed reception of *East of Eden* in 1952. Two short novels—*Sweet Thursday* and *The Short Reign of Pippin IV*—had sold well for a while, then dropped out of sight. And not even the talents of Rodgers and Hammerstein could salvage the musical comedy *Pipe Dream*, based on *Sweet Thursday*. Steinbeck and his wife Elaine spent a good deal of time out of the country in Europe and the Caribbean, culminating in an eight-month stay in England in 1959, which they regarded as the best period of their life together. It was not likely that his reputation could be recovered by a group of heavily censored wartime reports, no matter how effectively they brought back a time that most people would rather forget.

Not much care went into the preparation of the book. It is not clear who did most of the hackwork on the project, probably just office help at Viking Press. Certainly it was not Steinbeck. In his introduction of about 3,500 words, he observes that he had not seen the stories "since they were written in haste and telephoned across the sea."[1] (Some were written in New York after he came home sooner than the *Herald Tribune* had wished.) He apparently did little or no editing. He had an initial impulse to correct and change the articles, but he resisted because "their very raggedness" seemed "a parcel of their immediacy" (*War*, xiv). While he was certainly well advised in refusing to destroy their "period piece (xiii)" quality, the reader gets the feeling that even if he could have recalled all the details that censors had removed, he also did not want to be bothered raking up the past when his mind was teeming with new projects. He discusses rather sympathetically the problems with censorship and the constraints on war correspondents to say nothing that might damage national morale. He explains how this attempt to maintain an optimistic idealism was the reason why "when the war was over, novels and stories by ex-soldiers, like *The Naked and the Dead*, proved so shocking to a public which had been carefully protected from contact with the crazy hysterical mess" (xii).

One most enlightening thing that he explains about his own technique in his first venture into this kind of reporting is that in rereading the dispatches he recognized that one of his coy little tricks of the kind that all correspondents developed is that "I never admitted having seen anything myself. In describing a scene I invariably put it in the mouth of someone else." He says that he can't remember why he did this and theorizes that perhaps "it would be more believable if told by someone else" or possibly that he "felt an interloper, an eavesdropper on the war . . . a little bit ashamed of being there at all" (x).

His first supposition seems unlikely, since particularly in the climactic accounts of the liberation of the Italian island of Ventotene, one may wonder how the conversation of the participants could have been transcribed; although the report is signed by John Steinbeck, he is nowhere in evidence. One wonders indeed how a civilian correspondent could have witnessed such an obscure and highly secret operation. Information later came to light that the raid was led by the movie actor Douglas Fairbanks, Jr., —the only American to have participated in British commando attacks—whom Steinbeck had known in Hollywood (Benson,

529). Steinbeck had indeed gone along on the daring expedition and played a role in the liberation. (Despite Steinbeck's not wishing to make revisions, it is surprising that he did not identify Fairbanks, since the name of the still-important film star would have added to the interest of the suspenseful account.)

The second supposition, that Steinbeck felt uncomfortable about the job he was doing, seems in much closer accord with his negative attitude about talking about himself in public. His "little trick" was certainly "coy," since it accounts for a curious detachment of the author from his material that in some of the dispatches could raise question about their authoritativeness as first-hand observations.

He transferred this characteristic even to some of his most famous characters. Tom Joad in *The Grapes of Wrath* tells his mother that he is leaving the family not to become a visibly active labor organizer like Casy but to become a voice from a dark distance encouraging others. Steinbeck would not always retain this preference for remaining concealed behind his work. In fact, a major concern in a retrospective examination of his nonfiction is tracing his gradual coming forward into the spotlight, beginning with his first postwar reporting in *A Russian Journal*.

While these explanations are speculative, what is apparent is that when Steinbeck was finally thrust forward into a role—that of war correspondent—he had sought for some time, he realized that he had not quite worked out how to position himself with regard to the events he would be reporting and to the seasoned hands who had been in the business longer. In one of the most revealing statements in his introduction to *Once There Was a War*, Steinbeck observes that to the "hard-bitten bunch" of professional war correspondents who had been following the action for years, he "arrived as Johnny-come-lately, a sacred cow, a kind of tourist," who was "muscling in on their hard-gained territory." He adds, however, that they were helpful to him when they found out he was not "duplicating their work . . . not reporting straight news" (x).

This rationalization of his role long after the fact raises what is perhaps the central question about collecting these "period pieces" belatedly. His use of the term *sacred cow* suggests that he was aware that reader interest in his reports lay not in the limited aspects of the conflict that he had observed but in seeing them through the eyes of a celebrated author. The term *sacred cow* is traditionally used to describe something beyond criticism, though with the sarcastic implication that this assumption is questionable.

His insistence that he was "not reporting straight news" conveys the impression that he was just as insecure about his talents as a conventional newsman as he had been when he worked on Hearst's New York *American* back in 1925. He had put himself in line for this new job at the warfront by writing fiction and propaganda employing a large measure of fiction. Even the most gifted imaginative writer is not necessarily a newsperson—far from it, for as one of Kurt Vonnegut's novelists within a novel says in *Breakfast of Champions*, "The big show is inside my head."[2] Another possible reason for Steinbeck's detachment from the action he reports in these vignettes is that he is using fictional techniques to make them interesting whether they are eyewitness revelations or not. He is quite deliberate in positioning himself not as an authority on the war or military action but as a bemused and self-effacing spectator of the way that people behave. He will completely reverse this position a few years later in *A Russian Journal*, from which readers learn more about him than about those he observes.

One fictional technique he retains in the wartime dispatches is that employed with greatest effectiveness in *The Grapes of Wrath* and *Cannery Row* of alternating closeup vignettes of striking figures in action with generalized accounts of phenomena peculiar to this war—even this particular warfront. The dispatches are not consistent in style or intention, but they can be grouped into three large categories that may be called background sketches, myths and legends of the war, and battle actions. The last category is the smallest. Not much of the book is about the shooting war, although those pieces that are about it are the ones that have the greatest dramatic impact and that one is likely to best remember in the long run.

The book begins with background material intended to give readers at home a developing sense of the strange world that the servicemen and -women are entering. The first six reports, delivered from England between 20 and 23 June, provide a detailed account of travel by troopship from the long tiresome loading, through U-boat infested waters, to the long tiresome unloading. Presented as seen by a civilian interloper, the reports gave anxious families and friends back home a picture of what was happening overseas to those who might not be so competent to paint it. His minutely detailed account—with no names given— brings back vividly more than half a century later the characteristically boring and unnerving experience of wartime transport in often uncomfortable and uncongenial surroundings. Steinbeck's invisibility in these scenes proves a great asset, since it allows him to merge into the chaotic scene with the rest of the depersonalized participants.

Steinbeck captures a sense of this depersonalization as the troops trudge up the gangplank, heavily loaded down, with such a simple revelation as, "A man may express himself in the pitch or tilt of his hat, but not with a helmet. There is only one way to wear a helmet" (2). By writing day-to-day reports that took the same length at time to publish as did the crossing, Steinbeck managed, though readers were aware he had arrived in England safely, to re-create the suspense of a voyage across dangerous waters, the outcome of which is uncertain. (This effect is lost, of course, when the reports are collected years later.) Readers share both the nervous suspense and boredom of the voyage. Life on the crowded ship, where there is no room for athletics, settles down to sleeping, reading, or gambling, interrupted by the offerings of a small unit of USO entertainers, or to sharing tall tales and gossip. The gossip inevitably includes speculation that there is bad news that is being suppressed. In Steinbeck's fourth report, he begins to move beyond a description of the surface action into the imaginative one that the company is creating and to the first of a group of reports that today may be among the most interesting, the myths and legends of World War II, many of which may seem quaint to later generations. Steinbeck discloses that most of this "folklore of a troopship" (9) turns out to be rumors that some terrible things have happened or are about to happen on or to the ship.

Finally, however, this ship is unloaded without mishap, but with the same hurry-up-and-wait confusion of the loading. In London, Steinbeck must seek new subjects while he is made to wait almost two months for permission to go where the action is in North Africa and Italy.

He found little to report from London, shattered by bombing raids, or from a countryside crowded with soldiers. Although D day was still nine months in the future, the military did not want what was going forward to be shared with a tense world—all comings and goings had to be secret. There was action in the air, and Steinbeck visited a bomber base; but the action of the raids was far away in pummeled Germany. Even if the military had been willing to permit an observer to go along on such a dangerous undertaking, there was no place for any supercargo when every ounce aboard had to be accounted for in terms of expertise and destructive power. Having exhausted what he could say about takeoffs and returns in two dispatches, he turned again from facts to fancy.

The first of these, still one of the most enjoyable, concerns "A Plane's Name." It discusses how imaginative crewmen could not be constrained from expressing themselves despite the depersonalization necessary to carrying out military operations. Personal sentiment breaks through the anonymity of his accounts when he reports, "A rumor has swept through the airfields that some powerful group in America has protested about the names of the ships" (often those of sweethearts or movie stars), so that these are to be depersonalized to the names of towns and rivers, as is the practice with naval vessels. "It is to be hoped that this is not true," he concludes. "Some of the best writing of the war has been on the noses of bombers" (17). Here the instincts of the protesting novelist take over for the anonymous reporter to break through the bureaucracy he despised.

Four days later, on 30 June, he goes much further in "Superstition," an account of a tail gunner who has lost his "medallion," as the airmen called good-luck charms. Steinbeck goes so far here as to move from the third to the second person in his account: "You are conscious, lying in your bunk," that the planes are taking off again and will be for several hours as a frantic gunner, waiting to be alerted, proceeds through the darkness in the sleeping dormitory to find his lost "medallion."

Perhaps then he felt that he was interjecting too much of himself into the dispatches, for until 9 July they are confined to background stories about the brave resistance of the English and their relations with American soldiers. But then his imaginative power asserts itself again in an account of an "Alcoholic Goat," who has become not just the mascot but the "luck" of one flight wing. Something of Steinbeck's dislike of the high military brass that has delayed his movements shows when he observes, "In appearance the goat is not impressive," but "In every way, he is a military figure. He is magnificent on parade" (43).

Questions about his motives linger as one reads through the next four reports that reflect the same gift for satirical fantasy. "Stories of the Blitz" explains what people remember from those devastating days and concludes, "The bombing itself grows vague and dreamlike. The little pictures remain as sharp as they were when they were new" (45)—the whole experience is too vast and shattering to encompass, and one dwells on the details that pulled one through the experience.

The next report is particularly interesting as an early account of the curious history of a song that has become one of the major legends of the war, "Lilli Marlene" (as he spells it, the usual later form is "Lili Marlene"). His account of the song's legendary rise in favor does not jibe with later accounts, but he was surely shrewd in perceiving that it would become one of the lasting souvenirs of the conflict. The skepticism that he voiced, however, about whether an American effort to "turn the words against the Germans" would work or not proved too cynical; for what started out as a German song about a charming prostitute who makes her way through the ranks of the Nazi army to the top was converted—particularly in Marlene Dietrich's haunting renditions—into a key to the Third Reich's decline and downfall as Hitler's dream of a thousand-year empire was reduced to ashes in only six years. Steinbeck is right on target, however, in speculating that it would be ironical "if the only contribution to the world by Nazis was 'Lilli Marlene'" (47–48).

That his skepticism about the warring factions was not limited to the Germans is emphasized by "War Talk," mostly an ebullient tribute to the motor torpedo-boat crews (which he was not allowed to identify as the Commandos), whose "combined operations" did so much to soften up the coast of France and facilitate the Normandy invasion. The most cynical statement, however, that "there are more generals in the Carlton Hotel in Washington at lunch time than in all the rest of the world" (48), portends the observation of Ernest Hemingway in his 1950 novel *Across the River and into the Trees* that no commanding general had ever conducted the campaign from so far behind the lines as the one who went on to become president of the United States.

Steinbeck shifts from snide realism to the mystical in "The Cottage That Wasn't There," when a sergeant returns from a pleasant day in the country and plays the role of peeping Tom at a cottage he passes, then recalls that it had long before been destroyed by the Blitz. Steinbeck admits this is a ghost story, but ends, "I just don't believe stuff like that" (52).

Eleven days later, 25 July 1943, he introduces the character that proved the most memorable to emerge from his wartime dispatches, Private Big Train Mulligan. He appears in only two more dispatches, dated 4 and 12 August—the last one datelined London. A two-week gap follows and Steinbeck turns up in North Africa. Just as his reports were settling into a heavily imaginative cast, circumstances forced a switch back to facts.

Mulligan is introduced as a resourceful soldier who drives a brown Army Ford for officers on important missions and who "probably knows England as well as any living American" and also probably "more military secrets than anyone in the European theater of operations." But he steadfastly declines promotion because, "I don't want to tell a bunch of men what to do" (62–63). Steinbeck's dispatches share Mulligan's successful techniques for handling American officers and English women. In the third dispatch, he actually turns the narration over to Mulligan after identifying the story told as "one of [Mulligan's] lies" (83). It is about a fantastically lucky crapshooter, whose certainty of winning on Sundays is shattered by the international dateline. It is a tall story all right, but whose is it? Was there really a Mulligan, or is the story just one Steinbeck collected along the way, or is it his invention? He wrote others that climaxed in such trickery. *Once There Was a War* seems to again be moving away from military operations toward mythology.[3]

Even as he moves closer to action, however, Steinbeck finds another legend to launch, this one about the impractical dreams of souvenir hunters, particularly one identified only suspiciously as "Bugs." Bugs found a mirror, "six feet two in height and four feet wide . . . in a frame of carved and painted wood" that had survived a bombing in Sicily, and he carried it through an entire campaign undamaged until, when he was finally billeted in a house, he tried to hang the mirror. The nail pulled out and the mirror fell and shattered into "a million pieces" (125). Bugs consoles himself with the thought that "maybe it wouldn't have looked good in our flat anyway" (125).

Even after Steinbeck moves into action with Douglas Fairbanks, Jr., and his unit and the dispatches culminate in what indeed prove to be blazes of glory, he is not so much concerned about trying to give a panoramic picture of the action as to single out small incidents that stand out sharply against a generally chaotic background. As he had observed in October, "You can't see much of a battle" (115).

This emphasis on "little pictures" makes clear what Steinbeck talks about in his introduction when he stresses not wanting to duplicate "straight news" because he thought it was "the commonplace thing or incident" against the background of the bombing that leaves "the indelible picture" (45). He shared the old Wild West idea of "printing the legend," playing once again the role of a kind of Lone Ranger at the battlefront, seeking to do justice of a kind to the little people.

Steinbeck's final reports present the breathtaking chronicle of an outmanned but resolute force that scores an unlikely victory over a larger enemy force than had been anticipated. But, again, he constantly and colorfully interrupts the narrative with "indelible pictures" (though scarcely commonplace ones). In "Capri" (131–32), the commandos celebrate the liberation of the legendary isle of Capri by enjoying tea and scones with an Australian woman who has been stranded there. In "The Worried Bartender" (136–38), they take a chance with a captured Italian boat to rescue a bartender's pregnant daughter from a seaside town on which the German troops are advancing. This last episode seems so much like the work of Douglas Fairbanks, Jr., in Hollywood rather than occupied Italy that Steinbeck for once drops his detached pose to authenticate the scene, observing that the next morning, while waiting for haircuts, "We were sitting reading" (138), while the bartender appeared with Scotch and soda for his personal heroes, his daughter's saviors.

Even with his mask momentarily dropped, readers may find it difficult to accept a succession of such melodramatic incidents. Certainly it is difficult to accept that they were all carried off in the offhanded manner of a British "Carry On" movie. Even if it all happened as reported, Steinbeck was clearly witnessing the action with the fictionist's rather than the journalist's eye for good stories.

Finally, the curious thing about this collection of dispatches when set against the background of what we now know about Steinbeck's life is the tremendous difference between the reassuring image he communicates throughout the reports to the homefront and the shattered condition in which he rushed back from Italy. There is nothing here to justify his unwillingness to publish the dispatches as a book immediately after his return. While he did not always keep himself out of the reports, he did conceal his deepest feelings and reactions—a most difficult thing for an unusually sensitive person to do. While he was editing these reports for publication in the book, he wrote to his friend Joseph Bryan III of the dispatches, "There are many things in them I didn't know I was writing—among others a hatred for war. Hell, I thought I was building the war up" (*Life in Letters*, 264). He was then; but his friends observed that he was greatly shaken by his experiences and did not like to talk about them. One realizes in reading this book long after the events that Steinbeck was managing a detachment vastly different from the feelings he was experiencing. He was writing propaganda, not speaking for himself.

The book ends on if not a positive note, then at least a hopeful one (which may evidence that he continued to mask his true feelings)—on the same kind of ambiguous note that closes both *The Grapes of Wrath* and *The Moon Is Down*—that says the small gestures may finally make the difference in human affairs. The final conversation recorded keynotes the tentative but never defeatist attitude that characterizes the collection. An American commander is pressing some Germans on an Italian island to surrender and warns them that he has mined the building they are holed up in:

> Going down the stairs, the lieutenant said, "Have you really mined the building?"

The Captain grinned at him. "Have we really got six hundred men? . . . Lord, I hope the destroyer gets in tonight to take these babies out. None of us is going to get any sleep until then" (172–73).

We presume they got the welcome sleep.

What is the lasting value of these dispatches? What they tell us about World War II or what they tell us about John Steinbeck? They do not give us any big picture of the war, but, despite Steinbeck's coyness, we learn from these vignettes a great deal about the experiences he thought worth sharing. Despite his distancing himself from the action, the dispatches provide a personal portrait of a remote period. Despite his pictures of the depersonalized human cargo on a troopship, prenuclear warfare was something different from that available since 1945. This was an age when an individual—like the possibly mythical Private Big Train Mulligan or the Lone Ranger—could make a difference. Mulligan may have been a composite portrait fashioned from a colorful procession of opportunists that Steinbeck met; but the heroic matinee idol turned real-life commando hero, Douglas Fairbanks, Jr., shows that one man could significantly influence the course of events by outwitting the enemy in confidence games not conducted for personal gain. Such opportunities don't exist in nuclear war, for mind can no longer triumph over matter—or antimatter—once the firing starts.

What Steinbeck was actually collecting during his months in the European theater was reinforcement for what he had already advocated in *The Grapes of Wrath*, techniques for survival by finding a particularly suitable role for himself in a situation that confused and destroyed many others. Readers do not learn much about war, or this particular war, except in terms of general horrors that can be learned from many other sources.

One can sense in Steinbeck's adaptation to this new milieu talents that he may not have subsequently utilized to best advantage. The war dispatches are products of one of the peak periods in his self-education that in part enabled him to write his triumphant novel *Cannery Row*, in which he moves the reader with himself from the tidepool where death lurks to the eternal stars.

Chapter Six

A Russian Journal

Steinbeck did not return to reporting for four years after his experiences during World War II. When he did switch back to make a fresh start on his alternative career, he produced a book very different from *Once There Was a War*, different from any that he had published before. Much had happened during those four years to bring about an irreparable break with his past.

There has been a great deal of speculation about the causes of this break and its effect on his work, but the most specific evidence of the change can be gleaned from some of the least frequently studied sources: his two sets of dispatches to the New York *Herald Tribune* during and after World War II. The oversight is probably due to the long-belated general circulation of the earlier dispatches, which might be called "The Lone Ranger's Last Campaign."

No one of several changes in his lifestyle after the war alone accounts for the overall change. They were intertwined, and their cumulative effect made him an almost totally different person from the secretive, self-effacing crusader who wanted to blend into the action. Now he wanted to play an acknowledged role in determining the action.

First, his two sons, his only children, had been born during this period, and then his second marriage began to break up. When he and Gwyn Conger met they became infatuated with each other at critical points in their careers—he with her glamorous youth, she with his fame, hoping it would boost her acting career. Once the children were born, Steinbeck discovered he did not care for having babies around; he wanted to continue his restless travels while Gwyn stayed home with their sons.

But where was home? After the birth of the first son, Thom, the Steinbecks decided to buy a historic house in Monterey as a permanent home. But Gwyn had really wanted to stay in New York, and John found that he was not wanted back in his home country, so they sold the California house and bought a pair of brownstones on East 78th Street in New York City. This move meant a permanent change of lifestyle that Steinbeck described enthusiastically in "The Making of a New Yorker" in 1953.

Another problem involving this change of residence was that Steinbeck had used up the store of recollections that filled his most memorable books of the 1930s. After the publication of the nostalgic *Cannery Row* in 1945, his writings about contemporary California lacked the authenticity of intimacy. Moreover, he was never able to develop any substantial fiction from his stays in the big city, which were interrupted by frequent vacations and trips abroad.

With California exhausted as a source of creativity, Steinbeck turned next to Mexico and in 1947 published *The Pearl*. While this novel has enjoyed continuing success as a moral allegory, it has a number of failings. Steinbeck's effort to invest fishermen living marginally with middle-class American values aside, the remote setting, thin plot, and inflated style of the work seem a movement backward rather than a development forward in his critique of his own culture. And his next several novels proved the same, despite his effort to move *The Wayward Bus* from Mexico to a mythical California, populated with stereotyped figures from the past. When the Mexican government refused Elia Kazan's request to shoot a film on the revolutionary leader Emiliano Zapata, based on Steinbeck's script, Steinbeck gave up on both the country and the film industry for some time.

Meanwhile, he was being pulled back to the United States by an increasingly public involvement in partisan politics, which he had previously kept secret. His relationships with Adlai Stevenson, John F. Kennedy, and especially Lyndon Johnson became well known. By this time, however, he was involved entirely in national politics, not local matters, part of a perhaps not entirely conscious move to make himself a world-class player rather than a regional diagnostician.

On top of all these changes, he was also beginning to suffer from physical problems, which had required serious operations on his legs in the late 1940s and continued to plague him. These, along with other domestic frustrations, probably contributed to his increasing problems with depression and drinking.

When he returned from Russia, he needed to establish a new lifestyle that would complement a new form of writing at a time when he was possibly in the worst physical and psychological condition to do so. Elaine's appearance on the scene as his third wife worked wonders, but except for some happy escapes their world would be entirely different from the secluded one he had experienced with Carol in California in the 1930s. Most of his new friends were also celebrities now, and he had to accept the position into which he had worked himself, even if he found it uncomfortable at times.

The effect of all these changes can be discerned by comparing the earlier wartime dispatches with the unified text of *A Russian Journal*. Steinbeck's first wartime dispatch, reprinted years later in *Once There Was a War*, opens with bored, nervous soldiers at a port of embarkation waiting to be herded on a troopship. Steinbeck is merged into the crowd; there are no explanations of intention. Readers are simply plunged into the scene.

A Russian Journal begins, on the other hand, with explanations he had not thought needed before: "It will be necessary to say first how this story and how this trip started, what its intention was." He is sitting in the bar of New York's Bedford Hotel when photographer Robert Capa comes in. Both are looking for new projects, and it occurs to them, that, although the newspapers are full of stories about Russia, "there were some things that nobody wrote about Russia, and they were the things that interested us most of all"[1]—in short, the Russians' private lives. The bartender agrees that is what he would like to read. They call up the *Herald Tribune*, and when the editor agrees, they are ready to take off if they can talk the Russian authorities into permitting the junket. There is an element of self-mockery in this bravado account, but it is evident that whereas in the wartime dispatches Steinbeck plays the discreetly inconspicuous observer, in *A Russian Journal* he is a forthright presence, a culture detective, still avoiding politics, but seeking otherwise to ferret out what had as yet remained unknowable about the Russians.

He and Capa did not think they would be able to do the job they intended—nor did anyone else—but somehow they did, though not without enormous and exhausting difficulties. This time the dispatches could not be sent to the United States as they were written during the trip in July and August 1947. If they had been accredited by the Russian foreign office to send out dispatches, they would not have been able to leave Moscow; and they wanted to get out into the country and meet the people. This time Steinbeck had to take copious notes, while Capa took many photographs that they feared might never get out of the country. The book was compiled back in New York, where some sections were syndicated by the *Herald Tribune*.

As it turned out, they had difficulty getting out of Moscow because they had arrived without arranging for a sponsor. Without one they might not be able to go anywhere or meet anyone but other Americans. The proper agencies would have been either the powerful Writers Union or the national cultural relations organization Voks, which then had relatively little power of influence. As Steinbeck explains, "It was our impression that there has been some battle about who would be responsible for us. . . . And Voks had lost" (*Russian Journal*, 25). Mr. Karaganov, the head of Voks, was certainly not too happy about the assignment. He explained to the traveling team that other people had come to Russia, wishing to avoid controversy and get acquainted with the Russian people, but they had spoken to him in one way and then gone home and written in another. "If we seem to have developed a mild distrust," he summed up, "it is because of this" (25). Steinbeck finally won a promise of cooperation, but no guarantee that everything he wanted could be arranged. One of the most important things that the American learned from this conversation was the difference in the way writers were treated in Russia and the United States. (Something that he would later learn elsewhere in Europe.) Karaganov told him, "In the Soviet Union writers are very important people. Stalin has said that writers are the architects of the human soul." Steinbeck replied that in America their standing is quite different, "just below acrobats and just above seals," although he thought that this was a good thing (27). This difference in national attitudes he attributed to the Russians being "taught, and trained, and encouraged to believe that their government is good." Whereas, "the deep emotional feeling among American and British is that government is dangerous" (28). (This exchange occurred before the emergence of "dangerous" writers like Solzhenytsin in Russia.)

Steinbeck and Capa certainly did not get to see as much of Russia or to meet and photograph as many people as they had hoped. But they got further than many other visitors and saw some of the places they especially wished to visit: Kiev, the capital of the Ukraine, which had never been happy about its domination by Moscow; Stalingrad, the beleaguered site of the great battle that changed the course of World War II; and Georgia, Stalin's native region, which had not felt the devastating effects of the war so much as the rest of the heavily populated western regions. Vast numbers of Russians longed to visit this resort country, and Steinbeck was enchanted by it: "It is a magical place, Georgia, and it becomes more dream-like the moment you have left it. And the people are magic people" (195). This is only one of many eulogies that he bestows on what has often been before and since a dark and bloody ground.

One of Steinbeck's paradoxically greatest assets and worst liabilities was his naivete, which was to prove troublesome as late as his final "Letters to Alicia." He could be too easily taken in by displays of affection and too easily shocked and depressed by commonplace examples of greed, hatred, and envy. When he could not communicate with people or when they were deceptive, he was at a disadvantage. He was usually aware that he had to beware of confidence people, careful about exposing too much of his secret self. Shyness, in fact, was one of his dominant characteristics until his third wife, Elaine, by managing their public life, socialized him to a certain extent. On the trip to Russia, he was at a special disadvantage because of his inability to communicate with many of the Russian people. Neither he nor the multilingual Capa could even read simple street signs in Russian.

Steinbeck became aware through problems of multiple translations that he insisted on that what he said in English was not getting through to his respondents in the way that he had hoped. These problems became doubly troublesome in the Ukraine and Georgia—two places that Steinbeck especially enjoyed visiting—when messages had to go through two sets of translators, since Steinbeck's watchdogs from Moscow did not speak the regional languages, either.

The inevitable result of this linguistic impasse was that the book turned into the record of a search for mutual understanding that is one of Steinbeck's most superficial, though most seriously intended, works. Since he had decided that he was now obliged to step forward as the central figure in a personal quest that he hoped might enlighten others, we learn more about him than the people he wishes to introduce us to. Because of the language barrier, he did not actually learn much about them himself beyond their party (in both a political and social sense) behavior. We do become well acquainted with the idiosyncrasies of Robert Capa and some other American correspondents, but this text might well carry the title of Mark Twain's *The Innocents Abroad*, though here it would not be used in satirical contrast to the text. The book becomes largely a travelogue, alternating descriptions of much enjoyed festive moments with accounts of the trouble of getting to them.

Much of the well-illustrated account is about the only things that the visitors could fully share with many they met—eating and drinking. Steinbeck complains constantly about the amount of vodka that is forced on him and finally has to stop drinking. But he never seems to question how the supply can be kept steadily flowing in view of the poor state of the country's factories and drastic shortages everywhere. He attributes the bounteous spirits that flow in this dispirited society to resilience and never appears to question whether the national policy for keeping possibly disruptive visitors in hand may be to keep them tipsy, as well as sated with food. Toasts are constantly being offered throughout the book, but the conversation rarely gets down to what the people actually have on their minds, beyond hoping for assurances that the United States' aims are really peaceful. They really appear to want no more trouble with us, but not much of anything else either.

Much of this breakdown in relations, of course, has to be attributed to the lack of accurate communication, but Steinbeck never appears to get the point behind experienced diplomats' accounts of the behavior of Russians over the centuries in evading explanations of their behavior under the guise of elaborate ceremonials. Also, while probably few Russians were fluent in English so soon after the war, Steinbeck never appears to wonder whether more of them may not indeed understand more English than they are willing to acknowledge, since it protects them from running into trouble with the authorities while picking up some bits of information that might enhance the value of their services.

During his euphoric stay in Georgia, for example, Steinbeck encounters an excavalryman who drives his Jeep like an American cowboy and wins all the violent controversies he gets into with those outraged by his high-handedness. Steinbeck is enthusiastic about his performance and observes that "He was the first man we met in Russia who had the same feeling about policemen that we have" (171). If by chance such an observation had been overheard, it would scarcely have endeared him to the authorities.

His extreme enthusiasm for Georgia, despite its privileged status as Stalin's birthplace, could hardly have endeared him to his official guides. They were faced with the problem of not knowing the difficult, non-Slavic language, while the American visitor was establishing a kinesthetic relationship with his heavy-drinking hosts. Also, Russians who had suffered greatly during the war could hardly be expected to feel great enthusiasm for a region that, though it had lost many of its young men, had escaped devastation. His Moscow-oriented guides may also not have been pleased that an American—from a nation that they had been conditioned to mistrust—could write, as he must also have communicated through his behavior on the scene, "We did not feel strange in Tiflis [usually now Tblisi, capital of Georgia] for Tiflis receives many visitors, and it is used to foreigners, and so we did not stand out as much as we had in Kiev, and we felt quite at home" (156). There is a foreshadowing here of the movement of some of the former Soviet Republics toward the West after the breakup of the union nearly half a century later.

One could go on with petty examples of how the breakdown in communication resulted in this journey's producing little of value for anyone

involved; but there is little point, for today the book is among
Steinbeck's least read or valued works. It did not appear until 1948, long
after Winston Churchill had dampened a brief period of postwar eupho-
ria with his famous remark in Fulton, Missouri, that an "iron curtain"
had descended between the formal Allies, introducing the close to half-
century Cold War. Steinbeck's book was not reviled, as the author feared
it might be, but simply ignored. In an age when Americans most wanted better homes and better salaries, a better understanding of the
Russians was not a priority.

Indeed, in probably the most memorable sentence in the book,
Steinbeck observes, "We know that this journal will not be satisfactory
either to the ecclesiastical Left, nor the lumpen Right" (220)—precise
descriptions for the two parties that could never find the middle ground
of understanding that Steinbeck sought. As for the inevitable judgment
that this had to be a superficial work, he was the first to admit it. "How
could it be otherwise?" he asks in his concluding paragraph. The principal value of the whole exhausting trip and the book distilled from it is its
portrayal of the way the formerly seclusive Steinbeck came out into the
spotlight, which he would find ultimately could be a bit blinding. As
years pass, however, his picture of a Russia that few other Americans visited provides a peephole into the past. Steinbeck was not a stereotypical
American tourist but an explorer of unknown lands.

Although *A Russian Journal* might have started him in earnest on an
alternative career as a traveling reporter, it was followed for a long period by only a series of disconnected reports of visits to faraway places, few
of which have been collected. Not until after he had published his last
novel would he turn for his last few years into a substantial publisher of
nonfiction, although a number of the years immediately following the
Russian trip were devoted to a project from which one can learn even
more about the man himself. Readers were not even to know of this
most personal commitment until well after his death, four decades after
it was composed as part of yet another effort, which was not honored as
it should have been.

Chapter Seven
The Quest for Zapata

A considerable problem in dealing with Steinbeck's development as a nonfiction writer is that until after World War II he had made an effort to focus on his subject and not his own personality. Determined to keep himself out of his writing, he declined interviews that might inform the curious public about his private life. He wanted to speak only through his writings. Even after World War II, he did not want the spotlight turned on himself and his personal problems and triumphs. The journals he kept while writing *The Grapes of Wrath* and *East of Eden*, when finally published posthumously, provide a portrait of the artist at work that might sooner have increased both the understanding of Steinbeck himself and of the committed artist generally. Then, just after World War II, as earlier chapters have pointed out, a complex series of events completely altered his lifestyle and turned this shy, seclusive man into one who began to feel a social commitment that forced him to speak out in his own voice.

We have seen in preceding chapters the way in which Steinbeck progressively moved himself into center stage as a reporter, culminating in his expressing strong personal preferencees in *A Russian Journal*. His next move, though the boldness of it would not be made public for almost half a century, was to turn to history and rewrite it to his own satisfaction.

A supposedly long-lost manuscript turned out to be a narrative in the form of a filmscript based on the life of the Mexican revolutionary leader Emiliano Zapata, accompanied by a long introduction and running commentaries on the forty-five "scenes" written for Elia Kazan's projected film about Zapata. Steinbeck's treatment of this historical material provides insights into an argumentative side of his personality rarely displayed elsewhere, except in personal letters. It has biographical importance that goes far beyond its relationship to Kazan's much altered film *Viva Zapata!* which was released in 1952, just a few months before the novel *East of Eden* was published.

Pascal Covici had been much annoyed about the way Steinbeck had been distracted from producing this long overdue major work on account of his obsession with the movie. This first draft of the script is prefaced by a long account of Steinbeck's ideas about what should be included in the film so that it would not be merely a biographical tribute to a man he considered great but also a faithful picture of the Mexico of his period. Most Americans, Steinbeck disdainfully begins, consider Mexican history to be "a series of banditries and small revolutions and revolts led by venal and self-interested men," "comic opera movements of an inferior people." He set out to correct "such a misconception."[1]

Most of this carefully researched material was ignored by the filmmakers. Indeed, the film was not even shot in Zapata's home state of Morelos, as Steinbeck maintained it should be, but on the northern side of the Rio Grande River, near Roma, Texas.[2] This preliminary script is of unique value because of the insights it provides into Steinbeck's interpretation of Mexican culture and because of the forthright tone of his arguments. While Steinbeck sought even at this time to play down his role in his published works, he held doggedly to opinions not always supported by evidence and was not above resorting to high-handed techniques in an effort to get the producers of his works to handle them as he wished.

His introductory statement runs about 12,500 words; what he calls "a very full script" (*Zapata*, 53), much enlarged by his running commentary on his reasons for the treatment of each scene, is more than 40,000 words long, divided into the forty-five "scenes" (which in film terms would be called "sequences").

The shorter introduction is the more valuable part for the present study, as it is here that Steinbeck sets forth his detailed ideas on the treatment of settings and background characters that he considered of primary importance in creating a proper context for the action. The script that follows often repeats material from this section, along with complete dialogue.

Many of these suggestions involve the use of material and techniques Steinbeck had employed in *The Forgotten Village* to give it the air of a documentary while portraying a fictional action. He was evidently still annoyed at its slight reception and limited distribution, and he wished to take advantage of this more ambitious project under influential auspices to put across his viewpoint about Mexico's problems and their larger international and universal significance. He intended to do that by portraying Zapata as "a world symbol" and taking the action "out of the exact place of Mexico, taking it out of exact people" (48).

He sets about this purpose by opening his brief introduction with a highly selective history of Mexico. He moves from the fourteenth century, when the Aztecs consolidated their control over the region before the Spanish conquest, to the stirring of the agitation against the long and tyrannical reign of President Porfirio Díaz (1876–1911). This was followed by a decade of continuing civil unrest in which Zapata was involved. The turmoil finally provoked an intrusion by U.S. troops in 1914, but Steinbeck does not mention it.

This detailed account is principally political and protests the continuing oppression of the population by a succession of tyrants, beginning with the Aztecs, a rather small tribe that had battled its way into power and held tributary groups in virtual slavery. Steinbeck points out that the constant revolts of these oppressed groups produced allies for the Spanish invaders, to whom the natives found themselves again in bondage as the Europeans split their communally held lands into great estates. Steinbeck then leaps over nearly three centuries of increasing Spanish oppression and decadence to Mexico's participation in the revolts against Spanish rule that began in Central and South America around 1810, continuing for three decades until the new republics began to achieve coherent forms. (He does not mention the United States' involvement in this struggle through the promulgation of the Monroe doctrine in 1820, nor does he consider Spain's embroilment in the Napoleonic takeover in Europe that created the opportunity for successful rebellion in a distant and unwieldy colonial empire.)

He dismisses the intervening centuries as "a profoundly religious time," since the Spanish throne and the Roman Catholic missionaries "truly believed that their first mission was to convert the world" (12). Still, at the same time he depicts the activities of the throne and the church as largely ineffectual in their condemnation of the excesses of landlords, since "the villain here, as everywhere, and in all times, was greed" (17).

Although he honors a priest, Father Hidalgo, as the leader of this revolution, he actually says little about it or the republic founded by Santa Anna in 1823. Also slighted are the next three decades during which Mexico lost a vast amount of its northwestern territory to the United States, through not only the revolt of Texas and its subsequent admission to statehood but also the acquisition of California after the Mexican War of 1846. Steinbeck picks up with Benito Juarez's attempts to establish a constitutional republic after a period of internal warfare, but does not point out that Juarez managed to hold power for only brief periods; he had to fight off a French intervention that tried to use the U.S. Civil War to reduce Mexico to a tributary kingdom to France under Emperor Napoleon III.

Steinbeck rushes over the next decade of anarchy as Juarez strives unsuccessfully to get his constitution enforced and resumes with the emergence of Porfirio Díaz as the strong man of the state in 1876. Díaz retained dictatorial power until 1911, when his overthrow by Francisco Madero led to another decade of chaotic civil conflict. Steinbeck attributes the continuing unrest in Mexico (as throughout Latin America) to continuing unfair distribution of the land, but emphasizes that, like the liberator Juarez, who sought to establish constitutional government, Díaz, who reestablished and greatly expanded the power of the greedy landlords and foreign investors, was a native-born Mexican. According to Steinbeck, the problem throughout the nation's history was not—as in the United States—the destruction of an indigenous nomadic and pastoral culture by an invader's modernized urban/rural culture, based on European mercantile models, but rather the maintenance of an earlier medieval system of a ruling aristocracy transferred from Europe's decadent monarchies that inspired ambitious natives to follow the invader's authoritarian example. Steinbeck puts his finger on the exact trouble spot, as he had in portraying a similar system in California, when he explains that Díaz's method of pegging pay and wages at exactly the point where the bulk of the population "could not possibly ever . . . get out of debt." This practice, he points out, was not called "slavery, but . . . was a most effective kind of slavery" (24). He then turns specifically to a detailed consideration of the state of Morelos—a fertile area close enough to the capital to be kept under steady surveillance—where he recommended that the film be made.

The situation at the turn of the century established, *Steinbeck* then takes up the matter of greatest concern to him. "It seems valuable to me," he writes, "to put down a number of customs, habits, costumes, appearances of the people who will be used in this story, for the information of *both* the director and the producer" (28). His concern reflects the difficulties he had with filmmakers in the past, especially Darryl Zanuck and Alfred Hitchcock, who, ignoring his protests, misrepresented his intentions in *Lifeboat* and retained his name in the credits.

In the case of *Zapata!* Steinbeck believed the film should portray some of the customs and personalities of rural communities during the revolutionary period early in the twentieth century because they had disappeared or were completely unfamiliar in America. Mexico City, he points out, will be the scene of little of the action, which will be confined mostly to small villages where the natives are not descendants of the Aztecs but of the Nahuatls, people who built their identities around a close attachment to their communal village. To stress its centrality in their lives, Steinbeck wishes to pay particular attention to the importance of the annual fair on the day of the patron saint of a village, as it is through these occasions that each expresses its individuality distinctly.

In the United States, the emphasis of such fairs is on "winners," who move their prize merchandise from community to county to state events in search of larger prizes and publicity; the Mexican fairs that Steinbeck evokes, however, serve to maintain and strengthen local traditions. Although Steinbeck does not say so, he seems to have perceived the Mexicans' annual celebrations as rising out of the persistence of a communal spirit and the sharing of a culture rather than the one-up-manship of the increasingly commercialized U.S. showcases for the biggest cows, the biggest pumpkins, or the biggest gladiola in the country. Certainly this tendency can be seen as part of the kind of search Arthur Miller said Steinbeck was making to find a community "that would feed him, toward which he could react in a feeling way, rather than merely as an observer or a commentator" (Benson, 702), even if he had to look outside the United States.

Steinbeck seems to have felt that he might establish a strong connection with traditional communities in Mexico, but his attempts to get in touch with the scattered natives of Baja California, recorded in the log from *Sea of Cortez*, indicate a lingering sense of superiority to what he finds rather primitive people, as does his investment of the characters in *The Pearl* with a middle-class, small-town sense of values from the United States. Even in *The Forgotten Village*, he wanted to improve the lot of people with modern medicine; but his friend Ed Ricketts questioned whether one could introduce one desirable element of modern technology into a traditional culture without bringing along the others that might lead to its destruction.

Steinbeck does not appear ever to have penetrated and shared a traditional Mexican mindscape. Although he has some characters talk about having different "lucks" and notes in passing the wheels of fortune at the fairs, he never appears to grasp the dominant role of Fortuna. People feeling themselves to be at the whim of the gods are not confined by any means to the Mexican psyche but are endemic among constantly oppressed peoples of neofeudal societies who can see no way out of their plight by their own efforts. Acceptance of such a fatalistic viewpoint would undermine Steinbeck's progressive evolutionary viewpoint, as he states it most lyrically in chapter 14 of *The Grapes of Wrath*: "man reaches, stumbles forward, he may slip back, but only half a step, never the full step back" (205). Steinbeck's career was a dubious battle to reconcile what he saw with what he wanted to believe, to become a participant rather than a commentator.

Steinbeck's involvement with *Zapata!* marked a breaking point in his effort to become a participant in a caring community in several crucial ways, for it ended in his disillusionment with both Mexico and filmmaking after a decade's devotion to both. He never, despite his rewarding relationships with directors Lewis Milestone and Elia Kazan, had any faith in the Hollywood establishment; but he did believe that film had the potential to enlighten people and to alleviate conditions like poverty and epidemics if production and distribution were properly controlled. He had learned from his experience producing *The Forgotten Village* that even if one did control the production, one might not be able to get the product before the audiences one wished to reach. Then, from his experiences with the Zapata story, he learned that even if he compromised to some extent with the producers and other interested parties, he still had no power to get the film properly publicized and distributed—as he could do with his books. Hence the medium lost an auteur who might have made a far greater contribution to it.

Sadly, all of Steinbeck's hopes for the Zapata film were frustrated. This is not the place for extensive comparisons between his preliminary script and the final version, for the film finally turns, like other of his works, into a pseudodocumentary that presents us not necessarily with the historical Zapata but with Steinbeck's concept of a heroic leader of the people. His aim had been not to produce a meticulous historical record but a heroic legend. Since the final product was certainly not what he intended, however, a few important changes need to be cited to clarify some of his intentions when he was writing the original script. An understanding of these is essential to a rounded presentation of the autobiographical elements in his nonfiction.

One element that Steinbeck especially wished to exploit in creating a rich traditional background for the film is a *curandera*. This character seems oddly out of sync with his desire to take the action out of "an exact place." A *curandera* is usually a woman. She "does all of the village healing. She does it with herbs, and she does it with magic, and some of the magic is very old." He adds that these women have "great authority," functioning as a combination of psychoanalyst, hypnotist, magician, and midwife. He calls them "wild-looking," but insists that they are "great professionals, and except in matters of infection, they are probably good doctors" (40–41).

In *The Forgotten Village*, he had introduced a *curandera* in an important role as the opponent of the progress that threatens her power. The reappearance of such a figure in the Zapata script is probably part of his determined effort to share his knowledge of traditional Mexican culture with ignorant Americans. In this script, however, the *curandera* is not a meddlesome witch but a sympathetic, prophetic figure who appears at Emiliano Zapata's birth to predict, on the basis of a birthmark, that he is going to be a great leader. She also appears just before his murder to warn him that she fears he is going to be killed; but he rejects her plea to avoid what proves a fatal rendezvous by explaining that even if he is killed, "There are men, who, dying, have become stronger," like Juarez, Lincoln, and Christ, whose names Steinbeck notes Zapata is reputed to have actually mentioned. (194).

The woman is dropped altogether from the shooting script, which opens not with Zapata's birth but thirty years later, when he is part of a delegation from his village at an interview with President Díaz to request his assistance in resisting the appropriation of communal land by the great ranchers. His belligerence on this occasion results in his becoming one of the marked men on Díaz's hit list. With the elimination of the *curandera*, whom those interested in the political aspects of the story probably rejected as laughably superstitious to skeptical viewers, go also other indications that Zapata is in any supernatural manner set apart from other men. What Steinbeck had sought to turn into another semi-mystical Arthurian tale—like his first novel, *Cup of Gold*—became through the persuasive powers of Kazan and Zanuck—who won his agreement to changes—another tribute to the long struggles of the dis-possessed, patterned not after Steinbeck's *The Grapes of Wrath* but Zanuck and John Ford's film version of the novel. There the underdogs pursue an endless road while generations of oppressors destroy themselves only to be supplanted by new ones.

Steinbeck never publicly expressed any displeasure with the way his intentions had been overruled and his tribute to the indomitable human spirit politicized. He appeared pleased with the film, but not its low-key publicity campaign. He was upset when Zanuck became nervous about the political implications of the film at the height of Senator Joseph McCarthy's witch-hunting. The mixed critical response was also influenced by political considerations. Kazan appears to have seen in what Steinbeck wished to be a universalized moral fable—like *The Moon Is Down* and *Burning Bright*, set in no "exact place"—a parallel to the victims of McCarthy's crusade. Kazan himself had been called before the House Un-American Activities Committee and had to grovel before it to keep working in an industry from which many defiant colleagues had been blacklisted.

Steinbeck had warned against this kind of timely treatment of the material. He was particularly concerned that the handling of Zapata's

death by conspirators might cause problems with censorship, "for many
people of importance, who are still in the [Mexican] government, were
concerned in this dirty affair" (182). He counseled that no names be
mentioned. Kazan later acknowledged that much of the scoffing reaction of many Mexican filmmakers to Steinbeck's concept of Zapata's
refusal to claim power for himself was inspired by Mexican Communists
seeking to capitalize on the people's reverence for Zapata by working his
name into their propaganda.[3] Similar attacks were launched by
American Communists, so that the film was caught between what
Steinbeck had called in *A Russian Journal* "the ecclesiastical Left" and
"the lumpen Right." Consequently, Steinbeck's pleas for a compassionate
community were ignored. After these experiences and the Mexican government's refusal to allow the film to be made in that country, Steinbeck
avoided any involvement with filmmaking. Although he approved and
enjoyed Kazan's treatment of *East of Eden* with James Dean, he observed
that he had nothing to do with it, even claiming that maybe that was
why it was "a really good picture" (Benson, 773).

Steinbeck was disgruntled with not only the film industry but also his
own illusions about Mexico and a government that did not want a film
presenting a heroic Zapata distributed internationally. He had begun
having troubles with Mexican material when, for reasons that were never
explained, he changed the setting of the allegorical novel that became
The Wayward Bus (1947) from Mexico to a fantasized version of his
native California. He had also intended to turn the story of Zapata into
a "symbolic tale," but, as Thomas Pauly argues, Elia Kazan's interest in
the Mexican revolutionary "was intensely personal and had very little to
do with Mexican culture." Steinbeck's moral fable consequently became
"a timely movie set in the wrong place and the wrong time" (155).

As a result of his disgruntlement with projects to which he had devoted so much time and enthusiastic care, Steinbeck turned from filmscripts
and Mexican dreams to the "big novel" about the Salinas Valley that he
had been planning during his early years. Withdrawing for the summer
of 1951 to a milieu as far as possible from the sleepy pastoral regions of
the Hispanicized West to the starkly austere Puritan island of
Nantucket, he settled down—with long-impatient Pascal Covici riding
close herd—to write *East of Eden* in an atmosphere undisturbed by personal and political unrest. Even this work proved to be too much of an
unworldly allegory for critics, who wanted to see the old Steinbeck back
challenging the dragons of greed and oppression.

Chapter Eight
Journal of a Novel

Journal of a Novel, as the collection of Steinbeck's *East of Eden* letters was titled when published in 1969, shortly after John Steinbeck's death, is a very different kind of compilation from the daily journal the author kept while writing *The Grapes of Wrath* in Los Gatos, California, in 1938. (It was not published until 1989, under the title *Working Days*). Both were written simultaneously with his two longest novels, but thirteen years had passed and brought many changes into his life before he sat down on Lincoln's birthday in 1951, in his newly purchased house on East 72d Street in New York, to write *East of Eden*. The long-planned novel about the Salinas Valley of California of Steinbeck's youth would be a different kind of fiction from the epic *The Grapes of Wrath*, which he had written with inspired speed and accuracy in response to contemporary problems that deeply troubled him. Now he was to travel back in time and place from bustling postwar New York City to a pastoral community of the early twentieth century on the other side of the nation. Steinbeck's recollections of frontier days mixed sentimental vignettes of his mother's pioneer family with a wildly concocted Gothic tale of disasterous ambitions.

Unlike *The Grapes of Wrath*, this novel had been a long time germinating. On 4 June 1951, while preparing to move to Nantucket Island for the summer, he wrote that the design of the book had been made "long ago," but still seemed to hold.[1] As far back as 17 November 1947 he wrote to his friend Toby Street that he would like "to stop everything for a long novel that I have been working on the notes for for a long time" (*Life in Letters*, 301). In January 1948 he went to Salinas to consult the files of his hometown papers for background material for the novel tentatively titled "The Salinas Valley." With his attention diverted to the Zapata filmscript and the poorly received novelette/play *Burning Bright*, however, he did not begin until early in 1951 to make active preparations for writing, following the move to a new house.

Steinbeck wrote *The Grapes of Wrath* in five months. This considerably longer new work took eight and a half months, and then, for the first time in his career, he was obliged to spend several more months making cuts and revisions. Again, he apparently did have a detailed plan for the work in mind, for he often refers to matters to be treated in future chapters. Again, if this plan was ever put down on paper, it has not been found. *The Grapes of Wrath* had been written with remarkably few revisions, but this time Steinbeck had to make many changes in his plans as he went along.

Steinbeck originally planned to write his Salinas Valley novel as a semifictional history of the development of the region during his lifetime addressed to his two sons (aged seven and five when he was writing) to familiarize them when they were ready to read it with the provincial world of his childhood. He carried out a plan to provide a framework of letters to his two sons around the narrative. In this, he had planned to alternate chapters, telling the story of his mother's family, the Hamiltons, early settlers of California after the American occupation, with the fictitious and quite fantastic Gothic tale of the Trask family.

As he wrote, however, the original plan broke down, because he could not continue to alternate chapters from the two stories as the Trask family account began to require more and more space. When he delivered the novel to his editor and publishers, they insisted that the framework of letters to his sons—which had been his original reason for writing the book—be dropped. Although the original manuscript exists, it has never been published in its entirety.[2] Sympathetic critics have argued that the original novel was better than the cut version and that it should be published from Steinbeck's manuscript; but it is doubtful that the copyright holders could justify the large investment that would be required. Precedents for such a restoration do exist, however. Theodore Dreiser's original longer text for *Sister Carrie* has been published, as has also the original complete version of William Faulkner's *Flags in the Dust*, the first novel of the Yoknapatawpha Saga, which originally appeared in a cut version in 1929 as *Sartoris*. One difficulty that would be resolved by the publication of the original text is that posed by the entries in *Journal of a Novel* being keyed to the original manuscript.

It is difficult to match Steinbeck's entries in the journal to the published novel since he kept no journal while revising the novel. Little is thus known about what must have been an irritating period for him, except that he wrote to his friend the novelist John O'Hara that he "had a hell of a rewrite job to do" (*Life in Letters*, 432). He had expected to be able to complete the revisions by Christmas, but was still at work on 21 January, trying desperately to finish up in time to sail to Europe as planned on 1 March.

After all this work, *East of Eden* was not met with the intense response that had met *The Grapes of Wrath*. Perhaps Steinbeck himself put his finger on a major difference between the novels, when he wrote in the *East of Eden* letters on 25 April, *"The Grapes of Wrath* is headlong and I don't want this one to be" (68). *Headlong* is exactly the word to describe the tremendous rush of events filling the earlier novel: people on the move, reluctantly breaking old ties and facing unexpected obstacles in their desperate drive to find a new home. There is a lot of action in *East of Eden*, but it unfolds more slowly and often bogs down in protracted discussions, as in the passage about the meaning of the Hebrew word *timshel*, which becomes a central concern in the story. Steinbeck again exactly describes his intention in the new novel when he observes on 25 June, "If my book should be liked, it will mean that at last there is a revulsion for the immediate and a slight desire to return to the contemplative" (112). What he means by *contemplative* is suggested in the entry for 10 May, when he begins working on what he found to be the elusive problem of understanding the motives of one of his own characters, Cathy Trask: "This is a personal book. . . . I want the illusion of time past between the happening and the story to keep it from the kind of immediacy I am trying to lose" (*"Eden" Letters*, 80).[3] Contemplative readers might well ponder just what this rare comparison of Steinbeck's on the differences between his two big novels may have to do with the widespread perception of a "decline" in his later work. He seems to be striving for a deliberate, but possibly ill-advised change in his fiction that involves him in a struggle against something in the nature of his medium rather than just his own earlier techniques.

What is striking in his most highly regarded fiction—*In Dubious Battle, Of Mice and Men, The Grapes of Wrath, Cannery Row*, and the stories in *The Red Pony* and *The Long Valley*—is the powerful sense of immediacy that one also finds in the work of other great writers who have liberated readers' sensibilities, especially those in the American transcendentalist tradition: Emerson ("I am become a transparent eyeball"), Thoreau ("It is never too late to give up our prejudices"), Whitman ("I am the Man, I suffered, I was there"), Dickinson ("The soul selects her own society"), Hemingway ("I had made a separate peace"), Ginsberg ("I saw the best minds of my generation destroyed by madness"). Steinbeck's readers showed a preference for headlong action and a sense of participation. When Steinbeck turned more and more to universalized allegories, readers missed the qualities that had gotten them involved in his earlier work, from Jody Tiflin's beating a buzzard in *The Red Pony* to death to

Doc's quoting from the ancient Sanskrit poem at the end of *Cannery Row*, "Even now / I know that I have savored the hot taste of life."

Although Steinbeck continued to be defensive about his big novel, he may have begun to realize that the substitution of the contemplative for the immediate might not be the path to continuing success as a novelist. After a pause for reflection, he attempted in his last two novels to return from a contemplation of the past to the immediate; for instance, he wrote *The Winter of Our Discontent* during the same period of Lent that he was talking about in his narrative—although by that time he had perhaps lost his touch for immediacy, having been too far away too long. In the next chapter, we will find that in some of Steinbeck's least-known works, he seriously considered the role of the present and the past, the immediate and the contemplatively recalled in his own fiction and in other American writing.

Meanwhile, any discussion of the *Journal of a Novel* itself must begin with the recognition that it is not as interesting or valuable a document as *Working Days*. This is because interest in *The Grapes of Wrath* continues to be much greater than that in *East of Eden*, and interest in the journals is likely to be stimulated by the novels they concern. Both journals, however, have lives of their own that make them of value even to readers who might not yet know the two novels but who do have some interest in the man who wrote them both.

A most important difference is that *The Grapes of Wrath* journal was not intended for readers at all, although Steinbeck saved it because he thought it might some day be of interest to his two sons. He intended these journal entries as a limbering-up for a tough but usually predetermined day's writing. It is a remarkable account of an uncertain man writing a great book that he did not think would turn out to be anything like the success it became. The main note of the accompanying account, as mentioned in the preceding chapter, is the pain of producing such a grand-scale work on such a tight schedule. The *East of Eden* letters, on the other hand, were addressed to a specific correspondent, Steinbeck's longtime editor and friend Pascal Covici. They certainly would have been different in many ways if they had been intended for others.

In fact, if not for Covici, one doubts whether they would have been written at all. The editor thought Steinbeck had taken too long in getting around to this novel and thus wanted to keep a close check on the novelist's progress, especially after he took off for the summer to remote Nantucket, where some new distraction might appeal to him. Covici wanted each week's writing delivered to him. The letters did not go with these deliveries, as Covici was not supposed to read them until he and others at Viking were considering needs for revision; but when he occasionally visited the Steinbecks, he did get a chance to look at them and to discuss what Steinbeck was doing. This snooping at last led to the novelist to write on Monday 16 April, after Covici's first weekend visit, "I want to ask and even beg one thing of you—that we not discuss this book any more when you come over. . . . There are no good collaborations and all this discussion amounts to a collaboration. . . . And let's stop counting pages. . . . It's just too hard on me to try to write, defend and criticise all at the same time" (58).

Despite this outburst, Steinbeck was constantly counting words and pages. He wanted to keep on a schedule, but not get ahead of it. This constant figuring and endless repetitions of remarks about needing new pencils are tiresome accounts of the mechanics of the process. In contrast to the brisk, often cryptic, entries in *Working Days*, many of those in the *East of Eden* letters are long and meandering, as indeed the novel itself was becoming as Steinbeck again substituted contemplation for immediacy. On one hand Steinbeck seemed to want to get on with the business and get it over with, but on the other he often found it hard to get started and easy to stop as he tried to maintain an arbitrary timetable he had rather than respond to the stop and go of his ideas or energies. Still, he persisted in the belief that this was to be his "big book" (20, 33), writing on 2 July, "earlier work was practice for this. . . . And this is why I want this book to be good, because it is the first book" (117). Yet he seems constantly nervous about its reception and even predicts unfavorable notices. Then, a week later, he changes his mind about distancing readers and writes, "I want the participation of my reader. I want him to be so deeply involved that it will be *his* story" (123).

His attitude toward the characters he is creating is also ambiguous. "They are essentially symbol people," he writes on 12 March (27); but two weeks later, he asks, "Aren't they really living people?" (33). Steinbeck appears trapped in the dilemma of wanting to have things both ways, anticipating frequent later complaints that the two narratives about the real-life Hamiltons and the mythical Trasks do not fuse.

He justifies his design—"Maybe I can create a universal family living next to a universal neighbor. This should not be impossible"—as he begins to write the book. In these preliminary remarks he explains to Covici, "In a sense it will be two books—the story of my county and the story of me. And I shall keep these two separate. It may be that they should not be printed together" (3). Jay Parini provides a succinct judgment in response to this speculation: "Steinbeck did not manage to pull off what he had attempted" (Parini, 439). Elsewhere I have maintained that this dubious battle was lost because Steinbeck was trying to mix pastoral history with Gothic fantasy, "two seemingly antipathetic forms [that] can on rare occasions be juxtaposed . . . as Faulkner does in *Light in August*. But Steinbeck had not found the recipe."[4]

This is not the occasion to develop this argument about one of Steinbeck's novels, since the focus here is on his nonfiction; but since *Journal of a Novel* is the author's account of a great project that meant much to him and that many even sympathetic critics feel failed, we need to be aware of problems with the finished novel to grasp the significance of some of the author's uncertainties and contradictions during its composition. One problem concerns Steinbeck's attempt to moralize by having people drawn from his own family solve problems of "symbol people" he created. Moralizing is always a dangerous business, as Steinbeck should have learned from his experience with *Burning Bright*, especially if one is intent on doing good rather than depicting folly ironically, as Voltaire does in *Candide* and John Gay in *The Beggar's Opera*.

In Steinbeck's most memorable works he avoids moralizing and tries to awaken readers' consciousness to the possible consequences of immediate courses of action that are written out of his own observation of the situations as a detached but concerned observer. After World War II, changes in his personal life put him out of touch with the culture in which he had grown up. Arthur Miller's shrewd observation that Steinbeck wanted to be involved in a community "toward which he could react in a feeling way" is to the point here. In fact, some self-analytic passages in *Journal of a Novel* touch on this very matter. At one point he reports attending a party that Rodgers and Hammerstein gave for the successful launching of *South Pacific* and observes that he had had a good time, but even so, "a little sadness too because very deep in me I can never be a part of such things and I guess I have always wanted to. . . . I do not like the pastimes that amuse and satisfy others. . . . It is not that I dislike them but that they bore me and in no way hold my attention" (38). Even his problems with determining the nature of dislike here bring out his inability to find a community in which he can become involved.

A switch from his earlier technique of seeking to alert others, to wake their consciences and consciousnesses, is also indicated by a curious comment during his first week's writing in March, "For many years I did not occur in my writing, but this was only apparently true. I just didn't seem to be. But in this book I am in it and I don't pretend for a moment not to be" (24). This could be related to introducing members of his family into the story; but that matter is not brought up at this point, and it would not explain the difference between his involvement in the earlier books and this one.

Just before making this statement, he had written that *East of Eden* "should contain everything that seems to me to be true." Here Steinbeck appears to be trying to make the distinction, made by Wayne C. Booth in *The Rhetoric of Fiction* (1961), between the narrative techniques of "telling" and "showing." Booth has a "fine young novelist" explain to the reader, "I shall not *tell* you anything. . . . I shall allow you to eavesdrop on my people, and sometimes they will tell the truth and sometimes they will lie, and you must determine for yourself when they are doing which."⁵ (Booth is not, however, writing to support entirely the then generally fashionable view that "showing" was artistic and "telling" inartistic; but it is well to recall that it was widely held when Steinbeck was writing his postwar novels.) When Steinbeck says that he didn't "seem to be" in his earlier novels, he suggests that he was making the choices but letting the reader eavesdrop on his characters instead of commenting directly; later, he was directly stage managing the proceedings.

He had begun to turn unavoidably to the technique of "telling" in his nonfiction works, moving particularly out from the background where he placed himself in his World War II dispatches to the foreground in *A Russian Journal*. His fictional techniques had certainly influenced his earlier approach; now his nonfiction seemed to be influencing his fictional techniques. The different critical responses to the earlier novels as opposed to the later may be, at least in some measure, a reflection of the critic's judgment of the techniques as "artistic" or "inartistic."

The change certainly gave Steinbeck some problems that can be seen clearly in the passages in his journals or his creation of the character of Cathy (later Kate) Trask, who has been the subject of much discussion of the novel, not only because of her behavior but also because of her credibility. Steinbeck confides just after April Fool's Day that her characterization is going to worry many readers, "but I have been perfectly honest about her and I certainly have her prototype" (46). A few days earlier he had advised, "Cathy Ames is a monster—don't think they don't exist" (41). If, as has often been speculated, the "prototype" is his second wife, Gwyn, his further comment that "to a monster, everyone else is a monster" (42) is certainly "telling." Steinbeck disguised people that he particularly disliked as characters in some of his novels from *The Pastures of Heaven* onward, but he had never dealt with what appears to be the fictional transformation of such an intimately personal situation in such a monstrous manner. As Jay Parini puts it, "Cathy seems to embody evil almost arbitrarily" (439)—an oversimplification that raises doubts about the arbitrary handling of complex issues in terms of "symbol people," not just in *East of Eden* but in Steinbeck's later fiction generally. One of the problems with the technique of "telling" that does often render it inartistic is that the artist becomes so obsessed with the truth and urgency of his message that the reader is asked to go along on the strength of the artist's word alone, without enough information to make his or her own judgment, as advocates of "showing" prefer. One of the publisher's objections to Steinbeck's letters to his sons framing the text is that they contained too much "telling."

There is some evidence in the journal that Steinbeck was beginning to get himself too much into the novel. Only a month into the writing, on 13 March, he writes, "I now regard the book as the inside and the world as the outside" (27). Yet he did not appear able to stand this kind of total immersion after the move to Nantucket, for evidences of restlessness begin to appear as the outside world starts getting in. On 25 June he introduces one of the few political comments in the text by noting at the end of a letter a Russian proposal for a ceasefire in Korea and then adds enthusiastically, "I'm going to get into this thing pretty soon. I have lots of ideas" (111). Earlier, on 20 March, he had veered into politics to praise the Schumann plan for the financial reconstruction of Europe and concluded with a remarkably sound prophecy that "The so-called communist system will break up and destroy itself in horrible civil wars because it is not a workable system"—a vision few shared at the time and that took forty years to be realized (33). Steinbeck never had faith in Utopian systems. Every man—like the Lone Ranger—was on his own.

Ultimately, of course, the idea that *East of Eden* set out to prove was that individual salvation lies in one's own hands and must be found by enlightening oneself. What Steinbeck apparently failed to realize was that he had already explored this thesis in *Cannery Row* by dealing with an immediate world that he had observed intimately and recalled with luminous precision. If readers had missed the point there—as they generally did—they were not likely to discern it in a work in which "symbol people" overwhelmed the real characters. When Steinbeck went back to California, he should not have taken the Trasks along. Reading *Journal of a Novel*, one begins to get glimpses of why he thought that trip necessary. But was it worthwhile? This journal is not likely to lead many readers to the novel and, in itself, certainly does not indicate that Steinbeck was really in control of his work.

Chapter Nine

One American in Paris

One of John Steinbeck's most interesting experiments became his least-known book. It has been published only once, in French, although it was written in English and translated by a hired scholar. Some parts of it have been separately published in English in American and British magazines, but some have never appeared in Steinbeck's own words. Yet it is one of his most self-revelatory works.

Thirteen of the eighteen separate articles that compose *Un Américain à New-York et à Paris* were originally features written for a Paris newspaper to carry out Steinbeck's idea for turning to his own profit what he found one of the most annoying ordeals that often faced celebrities abroad: being interviewed about their reactions to the place they were visiting. On 27 May 1954, after settling in with Elaine and his visiting sons at what Jackson Benson calls "a spectacular rental" (750), a former Rothschild house in the fashionable part of Paris, across the street from the Presidential Palace at 1 Avenue de Marigny, Steinbeck complained in a letter to his New York agent Elizabeth Otis that when he did grant interviews they were usually garbled: "I wondered why I did not write my own interviews and charge for those hours of time and have it come out my way" (*Life in Letters*, 480). He was thinking about writing around 800 words a week. *Le Figaro*, a moderately conservative morning paper, much interested in the arts and cultural relations, with a stylish tone and sprightly editorial cartons, was interested; but the series was threatened by difficulties finding a suitable translator. At last an arrangement was worked out, and Steinbeck's "Premier dialogue avec Paris" appeared in *Le Figaro*'s weekend literary supplement on 12 June 1954. Steinbeck wrote sixteen more "pieces," as he called them. These continued to appear in *Le Figaro* for fourteen more weeks until 18 September. All but three of the articles were published later, at least in part in *Punch* or other London weeklies, and much later (from 1955 to 1957) in American magazines; but they were never collected in English.

These impressionistic pieces were not to lie buried in old newspaper files, however. In 1956 they were gathered, along with translations of five earlier writings in English about New York and England, in *Un*

Américain à New-York et à Paris, translated from the "American" by Jean-François Rozan. Little is known about this publication. There is no prefatory explanation, and no editor is named. The articles do not appear in the order that they did in *Le Figaro*, and it is not clear who designed the work. The book apparently did not attract much attention. No reviews have been located, and copies are extremely scarce.

The articles have been arranged to provide a kind of continuity, a development to the author's approach to the subject that he did not have in mind when he began writing them. Since an account of them in their order of appearance would lack coherence,[1] the best approach to these unique columns of Steinbeck's is provided by their arrangement in the book (which will hereafter in this chapter be identified by the short title *Paris*).

"Premier dialogue avec Paris"   The gathering does begin with the first article from the newspaper. Observing that perhaps it seems presumptuous for an American to write about Paris, Steinbeck evokes the memory of St. John de Crèvecoeur. The French diplomat wrote what Steinbeck calls the most faithful picture of eighteenth-century America because instead of concentrating on momentous events, he captured aspects of ordinary life that an American of those times would have thought historically insignificant. Steinbeck, who finds Paris enchanting, proposes to picture the city as he sees it and hopes that he will not fail too lamentably in the effort. Unfortunately, we have no contemporary Parisian reports of his success or failure in interesting natives in his perception of the city. He winds up with what constitutes virtually a second essay mourning the death of his good friend, the photographer Robert Capa, with whom he made the trip to Russia in 1947. He had hoped to meet Capa again in Paris; but just as the photographer was about to leave Vietnam, he was killed when he stepped on a landmine while covering military operations. No English publication of either part of this introductory article has been located.

"J'aime cette Ile de la Cité" ("I Love This Isle of the City")   The second piece in the book is actually Steinbeck's third to appear in *Le Figaro*. On 19 June 1954 he published "Que pensez-vous du Mac-Carthysme?" ("What Do You Think of McCarthyism?"), which contains his reply to a question that he was frequently asked about the witch-hunting American senator then much in the news. It was not included in the book, and it has never been located in an English-language publication. It will be discussed at the end of this chapter, along with some other pieces that were not included in his reorganized series of impressions.

In "J'aime cette Ile de la Cité" Steinbeck still appears to have some misgivings about the temerity of his undertaking these columns for a Parisian audience when he pays somewhat too fulsome tribute to what an American magazine entitles "Miracle Island of Paris" (*Holiday*, February 1956), an affectionate description of the island in the Seine, from which the city developed and where the Cathedral of Notre Dame stands. He brings his two sons (then nine and eight) to hear of the great figures of French history and to watch patient fishermen trying to catch the small minnows that are all that are likely to rise to their bait from the heavily traveled river.

"Sur les bords de l'Oise" ("On the Banks of the Oise")   This concluding mention in the previous article of fishing and Steinbeck's thoughts about playing a despicable trick on the Seine fishermen by attaching a fat trout to one of their hooks is probably what led to the first violation of the order of the appearance of the newspaper columns in planning the book. The editor skips over the fourth from *Le Figaro* ("Mon Paris a moi") and moves to the fifth, in which Steinbeck uses some observations of fishing along the Oise (a river in the countryside that does not enter Paris but flows into the Seine just northwest of the city at Conflans-Ste.-Honorine) to make some sweeping generalizations about American, English and French fishing. The article is one of the most frequently reprinted of the group, although it is one of the most stereotypical and superficial.

According to Steinbeck, "all Americans believe that they are born fishermen" and also conceive "of fishing as more than a sport"—"a personal contest against nature." He also argues "a nonfisherman could not be elected President." British fishermen, on the other hand, approach the sport quite differently, as "the English passion for private property rises to its greatest glory in the ownership and negotiability of exclusive fishing right," which finds its ideal realization in catching a great old fish and then mourning its loss. In France, however, there is "no sentiment, no contest, no grandeur, no economics," only "rest detached from the stresses and pressures of his life or anybody else's,"[2] a kind of fishing Steinbeck highly approves.

"Les puces sympathiques" ("The Sympathetic Fleas")   The jump from fish to fleas appears to have appealed to the editors as natur-

al. It was placed fourth in the collection, although it had appeared seventh in *Le Figaro* (31 July). This is also the first of two short stories that
Steinbeck included in the group. Certainly he is not reporting here, but
straying into satirical tall-tale telling, as he had in his World War II
reports and in the just mentioned comparison of American, English, and
French fishing. No English-language publication of the story has been
located.

"En quête d'un Olympe" ("In Quest of an Olympus")   The fifth
article of the Paris series in the book was the eleventh to appear in *Le
Figaro* (14 August), but it continues the satirical approach of the column
on fishing and the short story. It begins with Steinbeck's delight, echoed
elsewhere in this series, that he has received honors in Paris he had never
known in his country, where writers are considered successful if they
avoid entanglements with the police and sheriff's deputies. A new privi-
lege that goes far beyond his expectations has been offered him that he
make his own choice of a restaurant where he would sit daily at a table
with a good view in a well-lighted corner and could be seen writing a
world-shaking book by an admiring and jealous public. At first, he
thought the proposal presented no difficulties, but he found it impossible to select the right restaurant. Then he proposed that he offer the
restaurant an automatic mannequin of himself that would occupy the
table and write feverishly and sign his name on everything but checks in
his absence. He still could not think of a fashionable restaurant where he
would not be bored to death by the whole business, but his spirits were
restored when he thought of *Au Pied du Cochon* (Pig's foot) in the now
vanished Les Halles markets. "Let others search in cisterns of the mind,"
he writes in praise of the hearty fare of the buyers and sellers. "Here in
the great cathedral of the stomach I will make my home. My music will
be the creak of carts" (*Paris*, 91).[3]

Thus this essay, which had started out by continuing to enlarge on a
vein of satirical fantasy that was beginning to run through the series,
ends up at last as the kind of local color material and enthusiastic
response to the city's charms that readers had been led to expect from
the initial "dialogue." Only the final two paragraphs, however, are
devoted to this tribute that "Styles may change and the criticism of
today reject yesterday's great thoughts, but the carrot, the onion, the
melon, the peach, the half beef lying lovingly over a butcher's shoul-
der—these are immortal." This is certainly one of the essays that should
become better known.

"Des étoiles . . . et des hommes" ("Of Stars and Men") Despite this paean of praise for the old Les Halles, the series of essays tended to indulge in the abstractions that he said his sons were not ready for in "J'aime cette Ile de la Cité (*Paris*, 67). Indeed in the sixth in *Paris*—it was eighth in the original series (24 July)—about the only touch of Paris color is provided by the twenty-four geraniums blooming on the terrace where Steinbeck is watching the waning sunset with his sons, as he broods over with them abstractions about the ideas of universality that had posed problems in many of his novels, especially the recent *Burning Bright* and *East of Eden*. In view of the unluckiness of the boys in being subjected to these ponderous speculations, the title chosen for the American publication, "Trust Your Luck," not only misses entirely the echo of the title of *Of Mice and Men*, which dealt ironically with human hopes for reaching the stars, but seems ironic itself. Jesting with the boys that French stars grant French wishes, he suddenly realizes that by offering such dubious lessons, "we adults who have not even learned that all wishes are the same, moved by an imp, plant our own stupidity in children." Finally, after a long meditation, he asks, "How stupid can we be and still survive,"[4] if we call our common desires French or Texan or Pakistanian wishes? There is a nobility in such universalizing sentiments, but there is also a time and place for them. His series of articles had set out to show Parisians how their city was seen through others' eyes, but at the halfway point of the book we have departed Paris for the stars.

"Une histoire vraie et que ne le parait pas" ("A Story That Does Not Seem to Be True, But Is") The book moves from the stars to French history with Steinbeck's tribute to the national heroine Joan of Arc (17 June). One of the few reprinted several times, it was picked up by *John O'London's Weekly* on 10 September 1954 as "The Miracle of Joan." Long afterward, on 14 January 1956, it reached American readers in the *Saturday Review*, for which Steinbeck was an occasional contributing editor, this time titled "The Joan in All of Us."

The article argues that if the improbable coming of Joan could happen once it could happen again, and that any of us might be called on to play a role similar to that of the humble peasant girl of feudal days. Steinbeck's summary of the simple facts in a complex situation is somewhat overwrought and oversimplified, as is much of his later work, but he is clearly still pleading for a universalized sensibility. His interest in Joan is not just an appeal to the French reverence for her but to anyone with a Parsifalic mission in mind.

"Assez parlé du 'bon vieux temps'" ("Enough Said about 'Good Old Days'")   The twelfth article in *Le Figaro* (1 August) marks a turning point in the series. It was the eighth to be published in both *Le Figaro* (1 August) and the book. It is also the last of three pieces that have apparently never been published in English. The reason for this lack of interest may be that Steinbeck at this point seemed to abandon the original purpose for the series altogether. He says virtually nothing about Paris or France in this article but instead, in response to what seemed a casual inquiry, embarks on an intensive self-questioning, producing the kind of rumination on contemporary American literature that he had previously shunned. He returns from his foray into history to take a hard look at the present situation, particularly his own; and he produces an article that, though little known, is extremely important to understanding the future course of his writing.

The article begins with a series of the banal questions he is usually asked in the interviews he complained about, but he then suddenly takes quite seriously a question that an otherwise unidentified woman named Maria Crapeau puts to him: "Why are Americans writing more and more about the past? Some of them write stories of their childhood; others, stories set in the United States in the last century. Why write and read with such avidity so many historical romances? In a word, why are the authors not inspired by the present day?" (*Paris,* 103).

Rather than being put off by such brash questioning, with its air of censoriousness, Steinbeck is left speechless for a moment. He found the question more than just surprisingly pertinent but actually evocative of a reality so striking that it had gone unnoticed (like the matters that had attracted de Crevècoeur's attention in the eighteenth century). Because he himself could be accused of having recently fished in the still waters of the past (thinking probably particularly of *East of Eden*), he found that he could not pontificate on such an issue.

While he does pass judgments on some Franco-American relations in the rest of the article, he spends most of it in a castigating self-examination and a denunciation of many of his contemporaries. This may, of course, have offended American editors for the sake of their writers. While it is true that the best-sellers of the mid-1950s were bulky historical romances by writers like Frances Parkinson Keyes and Thomas B. Costain, the works most discussed critically were those by the likes of Norman Mailer, Saul Bellow, and Herman Wouk, all caustic surveyors of the contemporary United States. Moreover, the most recent novels that were attracting the most attention were J. D. Salinger's *The*

Catcher in the Rye and Ralph Ellison's *Invisible Man*. And Truman Capote, whom Steinbeck parodies as Joe Elegant in *Sweet Thursday*, when speaking of "rosy-colored tales of the little fairy at home" (104), was to provide with *In Cold Blood* (1965) a model for the literary treatment of contemporary confusions that Steinbeck mentions. It was Steinbeck and Faulkner who had become mired in the past in overwrought works like *East of Eden* and *A Fable* (1954). Most of the rest of this approximately 1,800-word tirade (more than twice the length he had set for each article) is devoted to trying to track down the causes of novelists' lack of interest in the present. After dismissing as a possibility the present generation's lack of goals and the fiction writers having reached a crossroads beyond which they feared to venture, he finally attributes it to a laziness that prevents one from making the necessary effort to see things for oneself and then judge them. All of this sounds more like self-analysis, however, than a recognizable picture of the contemporary American literary scene.

The most important feature of this article is certainly, however, his admission that he himself has been guilty of this escape into the past. Now, with this new recognition, he admits that he would be guilty of a grave offense if he did not fight against this tendency. Indeed, he would do this in his immediately following novels: *The Short Reign of Pippin IV*, based on the Parisian scene he observed in 1954, and *The Winter of Our Discontent*, written during exactly the period it is about in 1960. He also does this in *Travels with Charley in Search of America*. This effort was not conspicuously successful. Certainly none of these works matched his finest achievements of the 1930s.

Probably the reason Steinbeck (and others) had turned to writing about the past is that he felt most at home there, as he would show at last in *America and Americans*, the neglected work in which he actually speaks most fully and candidly about himself.

This supposed farewell to "the good old days" is, despite its shortcomings as literary history, uniquely important as a fragment of autobiography, for it reflects a course that Steinbeck would follow for the next decade, when he could manage to escape from the distant Arthurian past on which he was never able to place his final imprint. Maria Crapeau's question had a far greater influence on the last stages of Steinbeck's career than she could have guessed. The editors of *Paris* probably gave this piece the central position in their collection not because it appeared in the middle of the *Le Figaro* series but because it most vividly marks Steinbeck's change in direction.

"Un méconnu: le touriste américain" ("Someone Unap-
preciated: The American Tourist")   The following article in *Paris*
is the last one to appear in *Le Figaro* (11 September), as the Steinbecks
were leaving for London. The editors probably advanced its place in the
collection because it is the most striking example of Steinbeck's taking a
fresh look at the world immediately around him, as he had promised to
do in "Assez parlé du 'bon vieux temps.'" It is not clear just when
Steinbeck wrote it, for he was several articles ahead by August (Benson,
764); and he may have had good reason to hold up this essay until the
end of the series when he was leaving Paris, as the French might have
taken offense at some parts of it if they paid any attention. (Actually,
another article called "Le vrai revolution" appeared in *Le Figaro* on 18
September; but for unexplained reasons it is omitted from *Paris* and will
be discussed later.)

His subject is not a characterization of the American tourist but
rather the Europeans' treatment of the visitor. It certainly does not
repeat the usual stereotypes about overbearing Americans, and it is not
particularly about France or the Parisians. While it uses some French
landmarks to provide specific examples, it ends up another of his increasingly frequent pleas for universalizing experience.

Steinbeck's position is that the tourist is usually misunderstood and
sometimes mistreated, particularly because not all tourists are the rich
people of European myth. Rather, many have scrimped and saved to
worship at some of the cultural shrines of Europe. He admits that there
are drunks and loudmouthed show-offs but argues that these are the
exceptions and that most American visitors are shy.

Forty years later one finds it hard to go along with this sympathetic
picture, but the nature of Americans coming to Europe was beginning to
change even as Steinbeck was writing. Most of the tourists he observed
were middle-aged people who had come over for long and indeed often
long-awaited visits on the great cruise ships that were still running. The
Steinbecks usually traveled on these ships themselves. Flights were less
common and considerably more expensive than in later years. Paris, particularly during the August vacation season when the French flee to their
own resorts, would have hosted a crowd far different from that today,
many of whom were possibly nervous about their first trip abroad.

The great "rucksack revolution" that Jack Kerouac describes in *The
Dharma Bums* lay just ahead, the heady period of "Europe on Five
Dollars a Day," when the sedate passengers from the Cunard liners
began to be massively outnumbered by a younger set—many college

students on vacation, many, like the Beats, looking for an inexpensive, undemanding life. Kerouac and Allen Ginsberg made their first civilian trip to Europe and Tangier in 1957, and they were in the vanguard of many who would later throng to cheap, no-frills charter flights, bringing the junkfoods and soft drinks and other triumphs of American culture with them. Steinbeck would probably be shocked if he could see the extent to which Europe has become Americanized—even Paris, which has held out most strongly against Coca-Colaization and McDonald's dreams of a floating hamburger palace on a boat moored in front of the Eiffel Tower. (Jacques Chirac vetoed this proposal when he was mayor of Paris.)

But one cannot put down the suspicion that Steinbeck's feelings about the humility and shyness of American tourists are based more largely on his own hypersensitive feelings than on observation of his fellow travelers, not many of whom are likely to have dropped in at 1 Avenue Marigny. Indeed, his opening remark—"Now that I feel to a certain extent I belong in Paris"—may have struck both the French and other American visitors as somewhat arrogant, since many of them were not on a once-in-a-lifetime vacation but old hands more familiar with the city than he was. Even as he examined the present, his observations were becoming more internalized.

"Un méconnu" has appeared in English in both British and American publications with different titles and slightly different texts, which makes it impossible to tell which, if any, may be Steinbeck's original. It appeared in *Punch* on 26 January 1955 as "A Plea for Tourists." It was followed a year later in *Holiday* (January 1956) with the title "The Yank in Europe," and this version was subsequently combined with "Miracle Island of Paris," "Reality and Illusion," and "Discovering the People of Paris" into a single article, "One American in Paris," with illustrations by Ludwig Bemelmans, in *Holiday in France* (1957).

Some of the changes in the text provoke curiosity. The comments "The tourists practice French and Italian words before they leave home" and "Every penny has been allotted, every hotel price considered. Almost shyly they have learned about tipping"[5] appear in the *Punch* text and are dropped from the glossy American *Holiday;* but a sentence in *Holiday* at the end of a paragraph on tourist behavior in general—"A wormy peach does not make me hate the peach tree"[6] is not included in either *Punch* or the French translation. The most puzzling question, however, is why the French translator used *"énergie"* rather than the term *finesse*—common to both languages—when Steinbeck credits tourists also with "curiosity" and "interest"; both, like *finesse*, mental rather than physical qualities (*Paris*, 114).

"Sauce Anglaise"   The next essay in *Paris*, though it was published in *Le Figaro* a week earlier (4 September) than the piece about tourists, is not about Paris or the French at all. Rather, Steinbeck uses it to inform readers that he will shortly be leaving for England and Italy and to make some hackneyed observations about the sorry state of English cooking, joking that "I have heard certain treacherous British bemoaning the failure of Napoleon to conquer the Island because at least it would have improved the cooking."[7] It is, in short, one of the most trivial and far-fetched pieces in the collection.

"L 'Affaire du 1, avenue de M . . ." (**"The Affair at 7, rue de M————"**)   The next entry in *Paris* is the one that has become best known in the United States, the second of the short stories Steinbeck saw fit to include. Although presented with a somewhat diffidently straight face as an actual family tribulation, this is surely another example of Steinbeck's sometimes grotesque imagination. Originally the fourteenth piece in *Le Figaro* (28 August), appearing a week before "Sauce Anglaise," it fits as well after it as anywhere as a more extended example of tall-tale telling. The breakdown of the line between nonfiction and fiction is tested here as the teller is identified with Steinbeck himself, reluctantly revealing the problems that his family faced with a piece of bubble gum that develops a will to avoid its own destruction. Although the comic piece is too fantastic to believe, it did permit Steinbeck to add a long explanation of bubble gum to an apparently uninformed French public. It has made American appearances in *Prize Stories 1956: The O. Henry Awards* and in the enlarged edition of *The Portable Steinbeck* (1971). It was also translated into Japanese by Katsuhiko for *Gekkan Pen* (November 1969). Curiously, Tetsumaro Hayashi, in *A New Steinbeck Bibliography* (1973), lists only this Japanese translation.

The change of address in the English-language versions has never been explained. "1 avenue de M. . . ." increased the verisimilitude of the tale by using the Steinbecks' own temporary address in Paris. This was probably all right for an ephemeral newspaper publication, but either the Steinbecks or the owners or both may not have wished to have an address in such a prestigious location internationally circulated, so that a "rue" was substituted for "avenue" and the house moved several doors from a prominent corner.

"Mon Paris a moi" ("Paris as I See It")   The twelfth article in *Paris* is a very early one, which appeared in *Le Figaro* on 3 July. The editors seem to have wished, however, to preserve it in order to pair it with a later article, "Français, chers a mon coeur" ("The French—Dear to My Heart," translated for American publication as "Discovering the People of Paris"—perhaps Steinbeck's original title), which appeared on 21 August, as Steinbeck's most personal statements on what Paris and his "French connection" had meant to him.

When writing the earlier essay, Steinbeck was still fired up about the project and working at the top of his form. The whole article could usefully be included here, as it is not now in print anywhere, though it did appear in *Punch* (17 November 1954), with the pretentious title "Reality and Illusion," and later in the December 1955 Christmas issue of the American *Holiday*, with an illustration by the popular cartoonist Saul Steinberg. The article summarizes Steinbeck's intentions in the series. He begins by saying that he has been told that he has not seen enough of Paris to write about it, especially for a French audience. He goes on to do in seven short paragraphs of about forty words each what it might have been hoped he would do throughout the series—relating experiences meaningful to him—concluding "And I have lived regally too—have emerged from an expensive pleasure dome, accompanied by beautiful and sweet-smelling women and have seen in the dawn light the look of the tumbrel in the eyes of people going to work."[8]

"No Paris I can see is the real Paris except to me," he writes, just as all the millions of Parisians have their own personal and private cities. He goes on to say that because he does not speak French, "I can see a kind of Paris more clearly. I am not confused by words." There is no one real Paris, he argues; the city is what each person finds in it; and this is true not only of Paris but anyplace. Yet the city is special because so many people, not just Parisians, have found in it what they have not found anywhere else.

Still more about Steinbeck is revealed by a second part of this column that is not included in any English-language version, although Jackson Benson provides some details from the original manuscript (755–56). Steinbeck had originally written this continuation as a separate piece about his participating in a "Kermesse aux Etoiles" (carnival of celebrities—"stars" in the Hollywood sense) that proved a culture shock to him. He says that there is nothing comparable held in the United States. Benson describes the carnival as a kind of outdoor fair, "to which celebrities of various kinds are invited, each holding forth in a booth from which

for a fee donated to charity, they dispense conversation and autographs"
(755). Lawrence Jones, one of the few commentators on the essay,
explains that "the striking thing about this affair in view of Steinbeck's
usual distaste for displaying himself publicly is that he enjoyed it
immensely—the raving introductions and the autographing . . . he
wished that certain critics who have written about him in less than ami-
cable terms could have seen it."[9]

To get a sense of Steinbeck's feelings about this occasion and his
whole contrasting view of French and American culture, one must repeat
his own sentiments that he was profoundly moved by the extraordinary
occasion. He had never seen anything to compare with these thousands
of men and women standing or seated in the rain to see the greats or
near-greats assembled in one place to help honor those who had worked
for the Resistance. Again he stresses that in the United States writers
hold a much more modest place in the public's affection.

One comes away from this glowing account not entirely certain that
Steinbeck's striking contrast is entirely fair. He had had some difficult
experiences with hostile receptions; but he had never allowed himself to
participate at home in anything like this Parisian *Kermesse.* Although
there had been many complimentary and affectionate responses to his
work in the United States, he persistently emphasized the demeaning
ones he had received, especially in his home country. He appears to have
been especially well received in Sag Harbor, but he has written little
about his experiences there, and he spent long periods abroad during his
residence. In terms of Arthur Miller's analysis of Steinbeck's search for a
feeling community, he seems in the mid-1950s to have given up on the
United States (attaching special interest to his final big nonfiction books
that seemed aimed at reconciliation). He is much moved, as other
Americans have been, by his reception in Paris; yet he was not tempted
to stay there. Whatever the complex truth about a man constantly torn
between conflicting tendencies, this essay is a uniquely important celebration of an enjoyable public occasion. It is ironic that it has apparently
never been published in English.

**"Francais, chers a mon coeur" ("The French—Dear to My
Heart")**   As previously mentioned, one reason for placing the essay
just discussed in the second-to-last place in *Paris* was to use it as a
springboard into the last, "Français, chers a mon coeur," which
announced in *Le Figaro* (21 August) the approaching end of the series.
Though it is not the last piece Steinbeck wrote for the original series, it

was clearly its climax, in which the author announces at the end that he will never again be a visitor in Paris; it is other places that he will be visiting—"plus jamais je ne serai à Paris en visiteur. Maintenant je m'y sentirai toujours chez moi" (*Paris*, 154). Unfortunately, this lyrical statement was omitted when the piece appeared much later in English in *Holiday* (August 1956), under the title "Discovering the People of Paris."

There are smaller changes within the English-language text, but they are not considerable enough to obscure the essay's central point (a well-considered and convincing conclusion that serves to undermine criticism of the series as a whole, despite the unevenness of the weekly productions): "I had thought to make all Paris my field. I should have known better. Here, as in New York, my district has become my city. I visit other districts, but the place where I buy bread and wine for my family is my village."[10] He goes on to make other points about both tourism and Paris. Where he dwelled for a long enough period to feel settled remained a village, his village; but this Paris village was a very special one, and it was a long way not only geographically but culturally and psychically from the postfrontier Salinas of the early years of the century.

Steinbeck had, as the French recognized, joined "les etoiles." His Paris was the elite 8eme arrondissement, on the right side of the Seine near the President's Palace and the principal embassies. This article brings the series to a most appropriate conclusion with Steinbeck's discovery that he has been writing not so much about Paris as about himself and providing the natives not with exotic insights into their familiar surroundings but with an account of what a summer's residence in this city of light had enabled a celebrated visitor to learn about himself.

Remains of the Day   *Un Américain à New York et à Paris* omits two of Steinbeck's "pieces" for *Le Figaro* but adds five prefatory articles. New York is mentioned in the title, but only the first two of a group of five pieces are about the city. The book opens with "La naissance d'un New-Yorkais," a translation of "Autobiography: Making of a New Yorker," which Steinbeck had written for the *New York Times Magazine* (1 February 1953) as he was ending his fiftieth year with the feeling that he had in midlife made a break with the past and become a member of the metropolitan community. He begins with reminiscences of his attempt to make his way in the big town in 1925 as a reporter and short-story writer but had been driven back home defeated, and goes on to say how he has finally identified himself with the city after settling down with his third wife in a brownstone on East 52d Street in 1951. Arthur Miller, who had at that time only recently met Steinbeck, probably had this well-publicized piece in mind when he observed that Steinbeck sometimes thought of himself as an urban man but really was not. As we have seen in his last essay in *Paris*, Steinbeck himself had come to realize that he was only a villager in the city, that the inclusion of the memoir here is somewhat ironically irrelevant. He had been assimilated for a time into a village within the city, the East Side, a region where many celebrities and cultural movers lived.

The only other personal recollection of this period in the book is "Quand le printemps se lève." This title may be best translated by a phrase "when spring breaks through," from Noel Coward's haunting song, "I'll See You Again." When it appeared in *Punch* of 27 July 1955, quite out of season as part of a planned group of contributions, it was rather unimaginatively titled "Bricklaying Piece." It turns out to be one of Steinbeck's most charming pieces in the vein that might have been expected in the Paris series. It tells of his spring project after a long winter of building a brick coping in front of his New York home to protect a wisteria he planted. He becomes embarrassed when his work is inspected by an ancient Irishman who has been "a master mason for forty years." When Steinbeck says that it must pain the old man to see the kind of job that he is doing, he is told not to worry or be shy—his visitor is not there to criticize or give advice.

This heartwarming vignette has something of the freshness of his sketch "Breakfast" in *The Long Valley* collection, about a meeting with a migrant worker's family back in the 1930s. The next three pieces, unfortunately, were written in one of Steinbeck's least successful manners, that which he sometimes resorted to in the *Le Figaro*—that of the hackneyed or far-fetched tale employing a kind of residual frontier humor.

"Les stigmates de la candidature" ("How to Recognize a Political Candidate") argues that when a man begins to run for office in the United States, he begins to emphasize his role as a family man, to be nice to dogs, to stop wearing a hat, and, as Steinbeck discusses at length in "Fishing in Paris," to establish his prowess as a fisherman. The provocation for this labored work that appeared first in *Punch* (10 August 1955) was probably the defeat of Adlai Stevenson, whom he had supported for president in 1952, for he finally observes that Stevenson "wore a hat, had no dog, and if he fished, did it secretly—and he lost" (*Paris*, 45).

Even less likely to attract many readers is "Les marches de la noblesse" ("Noble Services"), which had appeared in the American *Saturday Review*

(10 December 1955) under the title "Why Not a World Peerage?" It proposed that men or women who contributed to the general welfare should be ennobled for the rest of their lives by the United Nations.

The final essay of the group is the most puzzling of all. The short, perhaps 800-word "Protestation et Suggestion" has never appeared in English or anywhere other than this book, and the manuscript has never been located. It begins with the highly dubious assertion that 4 million Americans claim to be descended from William the Conqueror and then shifts, apparently for no reason, to Steinbeck's obviously irritated observation that mothers are admired in the United States more than anywhere else. The reason for linking the two points proves to be to ask what all these mother-loving descendants of William the Conqueror would think if they knew he was a bastard.

The two newspaper pieces omitted from *Paris* prove to be better stuff than this, even if not so stimulating as one might have hoped. But they at least paved the way for one of his best and best-known pieces that just missed possible inclusion in the *Figaro* series.

Steinbeck may actually have considered the article that appeared in *Le Figaro* (18 September), "Le Vrai Revolution" ("The True Revolution"), as the capstone of his series. No publication of it in English has been located, nor has any explanation of why it was not included in *Paris*, although the compilers may have felt that it really did not deal specifically with the city—but then neither did some of the others.

Steinbeck begins by referring to an article in which the Communist party has identified him as an extremely dangerous revolutionary on the extreme right. He finds the Communists at the time of this writing about as revolutionary as the ultra-conservative Daughters of the American Revolution, because they value a system over the individual human being. The true and most lasting revolution, says Steinbeck, will be the day that all people discover they are friends and that each is individually important. He believes that this revolution has already begun, and he places himself in its service. Few people anywhere of any party were ready to go this far at that time. Certainly the revolution he foresaw is not far along. Although the Warsaw Pact Communist system could not sustain itself after the Chernobyl disaster, the succession of civil wars that Steinbeck predicted in a darker moment, while writing *East of Eden* (*"Eden" Letters*, 33), appears more likely to be with us for some time yet.

Toward McCarthyism, the subject of the second article he published in *Le Figaro* (19 June), he took a less confrontational approach than many apparently thought he would; and this may be the reason that his column was not included in *Paris*, although, again, it may have been because it was not particularly about the city; once timely, it was already considered passé.

The column was titled with a question often put to American visitors in 1954, "What do you think of McCarthyism?" Those who were asking were probably disappointed not to receive from Steinbeck the same kind of denunciation that other liberal-minded people had been delivering, but he refused to take the sensation-seeking senator seriously in the long run. He seemed to view him as he had the strikes that he depicted in his novel *In Dubious Battle*, not as the important matters in themselves but as "mere outcroppings that indicated the condition" (*Life in Letters*, 98). He had shocked his publisher Harold Guinzburg in April 1954 with a satirical poem, each stanza of which began "Schine and Cohn and Tailgunner Josephine/ Dancing on the Senate Green" (Benson, 748), based on rumors circulating about the belligerent trio. Guinzberg pleaded with Steinbeck not to publish it anywhere, and the novelist was shocked that his publisher was so afraid of the devious McCarthy. This warning, however, probably led him to tread carefully around the touchy subject, especially since friends like Elia Kazan and Arthur Miller had trouble with McCarthy's committee.

In *Le Figaro*, Steinbeck goes on to say that he sees democracy as an evolving process, constantly subject to dissension, but that he doesn't think these dissenters can actually reverse the course of a development toward a universal family. A menace like McCarthyism, he argues in conclusion, may actually be salutary, because it forces a democracy to develop its resistance, its vivacity, its integrity. Such a long-range view of a peril close at hand was not what people who felt threatened wanted to hear. It is not surprising that English and American editors failed to pick it up.

Steinbeck had not said his last word on McCarthyism, however. Shortly after completing his series for *Le Figaro*, he apparently dashed off what became his most quoted and memorable response to McCarthy's performance. First titled "Good Guy—Bad Guy," it appeared in *Punch* on 23 September 1954 and was not picked up by the American *Reporter* until 10 March 1955, with the longer final title "How to Tell Good Guys from Bad Guys." Despite this slow start, it became extremely popular as the tide turned and McCarthy's foes and victims finally got him on the run after his disastrous confrontation with the U.S. Army and his condemnation for contempt of the Senate in 1954. Curiously, although often reprinted, it has never appeared in any American compilation of Steinbeck's works. Perhaps it has become considered too dated, but its central point has implications far beyond the transient McCarthy menace.

The approximately 1,250-word piece is presented not as a story but an interview between Steinbeck and his son Catbird (John IV). It presents an interpretation of actual events as the impatient son instructs his father in the iconology of the old westerns that provided Saturday matinee entertainment for children from the 1920s through the 1940s, before television became popular. The basic point is that one can immediately recognize who is who in the movies because "the good guys" wear white hats and the "bad guys" black. Steinbeck explained Catbird's criticism to a friend who was a producer of successful musical comedies (probably Ernest Martin), who told him, "It's not kid stuff at all. There's a whole generation in this country which makes its judgments pretty much on that basis."[11] The Steinbecks were out of the country and missed the McCarthy/Army hearings, but on their return Steinbeck's friend told him that he thought McCarthy had been finished on the basis of Catbird's criticism—McCarthy came on as "the bad guy." Steinbeck then asked his son if he had seen any of the hearings and was informed that McCarthy was a "bad guy." "And, do you know," Steinbeck concludes, "I suspect it is just that simple."

Despite the popularity of this piece, nothing has been written about the circumstances of its writing. Jackson Benson mentions it parenthetically as a "marvelously innocent bit of mockery" (745), but neither Thomas Fensch nor Jay Parini notices it. On 20 September 1954, however, Steinbeck wrote to Pascal Covici from London that he thought a little piece that he had just written for *Punch* was a good one; his only original contribution to *Punch* during that period was "Good Guy—Bad Guy." He seemed quite pleased with this little caprice, which is one of the most delightful examples of the quick and crafty use he could make of his own experience. He seems to have been quite happy with his work during this period. On 2 September he had written Covici from Paris that "The Figaro pieces are completed in a blaze of glory. It has been a good series I think and I have liked doing it" (*Life in Letters*, 494). It was an uneven series, as his inspirations waxed and wanted; but the best pieces are among some of his most thoughtful and self-revealing. They deserve to be better known.

Chapter Ten

Travels with Charley in Search of America

The impetus for *Travels with Charley in Search of America* can surely be traced back to Steinbeck's interview with Maria Crapeau in Paris in 1954, during which she asked Steinbeck why Americans write more and more about the past. Although he could not settle on any overall explanation, he did say that as far as he was concerned, he had been so much absorbed in his work that he was unconscious of this tendency; now that it had been called to his attention, however, he promised to fight against it—as he did in his next two novels, fables about moral decay in contemporary France (*The Short Reign of Pippin IV*) and the United States (*The Winter of Our Discontent*).

While he was working on this last novel in 1960, he began to think seriously about the trip around the United States that his agent Elizabeth Otis had long been urging him to take. Having been outside the country for long periods, he felt he had lost "the flavor and touch and sound of it," as he wrote to musical comedy composer Frank Loesser (*Life in Letters*, 666). When Steinbeck announced his proposed mode of travel, Otis, his wife, and his publisher were upset. In a letter to Otis, he pointed out that he wanted to avoid motels and bus routes on the main highways. He intended instead to have a special vehicle built for him, a kind of camper mounted on a truck body—sort of a glorified version of the hybrid machines the Okies had invented for their perilous trips to the West. This would enable him to be self-sufficient and to get into the countryside, so that he could see "people not in movement but at home in their own places" (*Life in Letters*, 668–69). Since his associates thought this whole scheme "quixotic," he named the vehicle Rocinante, after Don Quixote's horse. As his Sancho Panza, he chose the giant "blue" poodle Charley, named in the title. Steinbeck loosely modeled the book after *Travels with a Donkey* by Robert Louis Stevenson, one of Steinbeck's favorite authors. Stevenson's trip through the wild mountains of France in the nineteenth century was, however, a far different, more romantic journey, which did not bring him in touch with disheartening realities.

Steinbeck had intended to leave just after Labor Day, when the summer tourists would be off the road and children back in school, but his departure was delayed by Hurricane Donna, which devastated Sag Harbor. He managed to save both his boat and Rocinante, and then set off on Saturday, 23 September 1960.

The book is divided into four unequal parts. The first is only fourteen pages and explains the preparations for the trip. Part 2, which is just short of a hundred pages, takes up about 30 percent of the narrative but moves him only from Long Island by ferry into New England and on to the Canadian border on a winding trip through what he found the fascinating state of Maine. He then speeds up to Chicago for a first meeting with his wife Elaine, a period of only seventeen days of a three-month trip.

As the book has now become a period piece, one must steadily bear in mind that the trip was made during the last months of the John F. Kennedy/Richard Nixon campaigns for the presidency. Steinbeck found people willing to comment on local issues but reluctant to commit themselves on their preference in the hard-fought and often vitriolic campaign that ended in only a tiny margin of victory for Kennedy. (Steinbeck never comments on the outcome of the campaign, though he was still on the road when it occurred.)

It is equally important to bear in mind that the traveler's United States in 1960 was very different logistically from the one that greets wanderers today. The vast interstate highway system, which President Eisenhower had campaigned for successfully on the basis of its usefulness to the national defense, was just beginning to get Americans on the road for longer journeys in the Midwest and West. Few stretches yet existed in the South or in the crowded East, where building costs were higher. There were some pioneering toll roads, such as the Pennsylvania Turnpike, that Steinbeck used to speed his way home once he became travel weary, but because of his preference for back roads, Rocinante was often slowed down by congested traffic and speed traps in small towns. This was especially true in the South, which depended on fines for its civic expenditures and where backwoods legislators were desperately fighting to keep from being bypassed by the two-track speedways.

The first leg of the journey, about his week in the nearly deserted regions of northern Maine, is recorded in greatest detail. He then spends five pages on an altercation with American border guards at Niagara Falls, where he had planned to cross the southern part of Canada to avoid the crowded roads on the south side of Lake Erie. His plan is thwarted because of his failure to have renewed Charley's rabies vaccination. Although the fault is Steinbeck's, this passing incident provided one of the infrequent insights into an aspect of his character, as he rages about his grievance of admiring "all nations" and hating "all governments" because "government can make you feel so small and mean that it takes some doing to build back a sense of self-importance" (*Travels*, 85). Although Steinbeck did not want to be recognized on this trip so that he could get people to talk freely to him, one gets a sense that he was disproportionately annoyed by this border incident because the government officials did not recognize his name. The detailed account is particularly arresting because few other conversations are reported in such detail.

Part 3 begins with his departure from Chicago, where he says little about the reunion with his wife but does enjoy getting back to the comforts of a hotel room. Because such luxurious days off the road broke the continuity of his trip and such a break is "possible in life but not in writing" (*Travels*, 123), he leaves the city, as he will many other places, without smoothing over the gap. This hundred-page section begins with the abrupt takeoff from Chicago and ends about six weeks later in a conversation with Charley while they spend the night in Rocinante on New Mexico's Continental Divide. This comes after one of the most trying experiences of his campaign, a return to his native region of California, which had received *East of Eden* little better than it had *The Grapes of Wrath*. Steinbeck is much more useful to the local chamber of commerce as a statue that attracts tourists than as an angry presence.

The major conversation he recalls between crossing the Mississippi River and reaching the Pacific Coast in Seattle, where Elaine joined him again, occurred after he crossed the Great Divide in Idaho and holed up for the night in an otherwise untenanted tourist court. Here he became involved in a dispute between the burly owner of this desolate outpost—a backwoods type who liked hunting and fishing and drinking—and the owner's twenty-year-old son, who has taken an evening course in hairdressing and now wants to try his hand in town. The father had expected the son would "just finish high school and that would be the end of it" (173); and he is particularly upset about his son's choosing what he considers an effeminate calling. Steinbeck, reluctant to serve as arbiter, diplomatically comforts the ambitious boy, who offers his "considered opinion that the hairdresser is the most influential man in any community" (174).

At last he gets back to Monterey for a touching reunion with old friends, who insist that he must stay there with them; but he feels that he is now more of a ghost there than those who have actually died. The town has changed, and Steinbeck has changed, and the changes have had the effect of alienating them. After an enthusiastic period of sharing memories, he realizes, "My return caused only confusion and uneasiness. . . . Tom Wolfe was right. You can't go home again because home has ceased to exist except in the mothballs of memory" (205). He decides to leave not just Cannery Row but California itself by the quickest route possible, over the mountains, through the frightening desert, and on to Texas. He has not gotten on any better with his conservative remaining family members than with his rowdy old buddies.

Part 4 is fifty pages long and consists almost entirely of reconstructions of two scenes presented in the greatest detail of any in the book, as he visits with Elaine's friends and relatives in Texas over Thanksgiving and then moves out by himself to a chilling December encounter in New Orleans.

He did not intend to dwell long on Texas, but he does, in a section joltingly out of character with the tone and style of the rest of the book. For the first time in his long trip, he is in a place where he really feels at home; and he does not know quite how to handle his changed relationship to the reader. He seems to feel that since he has been constantly on the defensive in the book, he must remain so; but he chooses an awkward and unconvincing way to do it. He finds he really likes the Texans, so that he must take up for them against imagined critics.

He begins his leisurely reminiscence of an expansive but basically unostentatious lifestyle with eight pages of hackneyed generalities about Texas, arguing that it is more than a state of mind, "It is a mystique closely approximating a religion" (227). Such statements may leave readers skeptical, although his intention seems not to be to satirize the Texans so much as the outsiders to whom the state has become a symbol for extravagant lifestyles. His tone is illustrated in the statement, "no account of Texas would be complete without a Texas orgy, showing men of great wealth squandering their millions on tasteless and impassioned exhibitionism" (233). He is writing almost two decades before the nighttime soap opera *Dallas* made Texas an international symbol of vast wealth and decadent power. Although he never mentions Edna Ferber's novel *Giant* (1952) and its lavish film version (1956) starring cult hero James Dean, the film would still have been familiar to vast audiences in the 1960s at the time the continued rise of Lyndon Johnson was giving Texas an increasingly powerful role in national and world affairs.

In describing his experiences with Texas hospitality, Steinbeck tries to deflate the myths of flaunting riches and orgiastic decadence by giving his account of sharing a genial domestic festival with good plain folks. His tone is suggested by his comment, "How unthinkably rich these Texans must be to live as simply as they were" (236). His intention is clear, but his approach is heavy-handed, as it is at times in the *Le Figaro* series and in the bitterly satirical "The Short-Short Story of Mankind" (1958). It's not quite clear whether he is overstating his own case or that of other critics. The account might make its point better as simply his own full sharing of one good time on a trip that did not seem to have produced many. Changing from straightforward narrative to tongue-in-cheek hyperbole at the end of a long personal account of this kind can confuse readers. Taken as it seems to have been intended, one still concludes that this episode is almost embarrassingly overstated; but one of the most diffiicult things to do is to rescue those who deserve better from stereotypes without becoming fulsome.

The defense of Texas also provides an off-key lead to what is generally acknowledged to be the most powerful and distressing episode of the book—the account of Steinbeck's visit to New Orleans to see for himself the behavior of the "Cheerleaders," a group of white mothers who were protesting the admission of black children to the previously segregated public schools. After witnessing the venomous torrents of scurrilous language unleashed at one little black girl, what made him "sick with nausea" is that the women's language expresses not "a spontaneous cry of anger, of insane rage" but the deliberate tactics of "blowzy women who hungered for attention, wanted to be admired" (256). When he later meets a rational native white who asks Steinbeck if he is traveling for pleasure, he replies, "I was until today. I saw the Cheerleaders." Later attempts to interview black people produce less satisfying results. He gives an older man a lift in Rocinante but the man is afraid to talk at all. A young black student talks freely and argues that Martin Luther King's method is too slow. He wants action right now. Meanwhile, Steinbeck has been denounced as a "Commie nigger-lover" by a towheaded white man who begs a ride and then denounces "trouble-makers—come down here and tell us how to live." This man praises the Cheerleaders—"Does your heart good to see somebody do their duty" (268–69). Steinbeck orders him out of the car and speeds away. And with this last brief encounter he wishes his journey was over, while he still has miles to go to home.

There had been complaints about the book ending abruptly, without a conclusion, but Steinbeck had done this before, in his first personal narrative, the log from *Sea of Cortez*. He was as anxious to end the books as he had been to end the trips once the mission was completed. In

Travels with Charley, however, he offers tentative conclusions along the way. His record stops where it should. He has taken the reader with him—at least on segments of the trip; and he has shared all that he plans. At first, evidently, the book did push beyond the point of his getting nearly home; Jackson Benson quotes from the manuscript a passage about the Steinbecks attending John F. Kennedy's inauguration with Kenneth Galbraith and his wife, but gives no further indication of how extensive the cuts may have been.

What is also known is that Steinbeck included in his manuscript some of the actual scurrilous language used by the New Orleans Cheerleaders, but his publisher was nervous about including it because of fears of censorship and court cases. Cases involving D. H. Lawrence's *Lady Chatterley's Lover* and Henry Miller's *Tropic of Cancer* were still being tried and were bankrupting Barney Rosset's Grove Press, despite its vindication. Viking warned that Steinbeck would have to handle any action on his own. When going over the proofs, he finally decided that his point could be made without actually quoting the language.

In the very closing scene in the book, Steinbeck pulls up at the curb in a no-parking area in New York City and tells "an old-fashioned cop" that he is lost in his own town (275). One might borrow the title from the motion picture made many years later, *Lost in America*, to show how long the condition in which he found himself continued. He had found fragments of a country, but not what he wanted to find. In fact, except during the holiday in Texas that provided him with an enjoyable interlude, he did not like much of what he had found. What he had hoped to find would be spelled out specifically in his last book, *America and Americans* (1966), an unexpected spinoff from *Travels with Charley*, along with an admission that he could offer no prescription for finding it.

Travels with Charley is the only one of Steinbeck's autobiographical works to develop a critical literature of its own, although it speaks quite plainly for itself. Much has been written about the log from *Sea of Cortez*, but with a focus on Ed Ricketts's non-teleological philosophy. There has been little effort to discern any "design" of Steinbeck's that may have escaped detection. The writing about *Travels with Charley*, however, focuses on Steinbeck's intentions and achievements, beginning with John Ditsky's "The Quest that Failed" (1975). Support for his title can certainly be found in the observation Steinbeck made when he got back to his native California: "We have overcome all enemies but ourselves" (196). It echoes the proclamation of the possum-hero of Walt Kelly's then popular comic strip, *Pogo*, who said: "We have met the enemy, and he is us."

Ditsky builds on Steinbeck's naming his curious vehicle Rocinante and his titling in military fashion the trip itself—"Operation Windmills"—commenting that "it is the monster America that wins in the end sending the potentially comic adventurers home in full retreat. It is not really laughable after all; it comes closest to unintended pathos."[1] This interpretation is reinforced by Richard Astro's "Travels with Steinbeck," which looks only briefly at *Travels* in connection with other travel works and links it with *Sea of Cortez*, seeing both as records of "significant and important journeys." Astro praises the *Travels* particularly for presenting "an image of loss by a writer whose most cherished beliefs had come to haunt him." He finds the book "a wasteland vision," "a series of fragments he has shored against his ruins."[2]

Putting aside Paul McCarthy's objection to describing Steinbeck as possessing a "wasteland vision,"[3] Ditsky and Astro are well justified in associating him temperamentally with the Eliot/Fitzgerald generation. There is throughout his work—even his upbeat later writings—a pervading sense of waste: wasted hopes, wasted energies, wasted efforts. *Travels with Charley* is finally a melancholy chronicle about someone who sets out to find America and gets lost himself in a literal as well as a metaphorical sense.

After setting down the account of his travels, Steinbeck might very well have pondered the example of J. D. Salinger, another visionary with whom he had much in common,[4] who, having written himself into a restful stasis, retired. Steinbeck decided, however, not to rest on his laurels but, like Tennyson's Ulysses, to take to the road once more. He might have spent his last days in Sag Harbor or even back in Somerset, continuing his endless task of resurrecting the shadowy King Arthur by summoning him up in the exploding light of a modern wasteland. Instead, he lured himself into making the most disastrous mistake of a career marked by many happy accidents but also marred by many missteps.

Now that we are distanced enough from the time of the *Travels* to see the book as a period piece, the principal question that comes to mind is why it was so popular when it was published. It enjoyed the greatest sale during the first few months it was in print of any of Steinbeck's books, surpassing even the record sales of *The Grapes of Wrath*, though *Travels* has not sustained this lead over the years. Its reception is surprising, because it is certainly not the kind of optimistic, upbeat book (such as Dale Carnegie's *How to Win Friends and Influence People*) that usually captivates a huge American audience.

The quality of the book that reviewers most often praised was its honesty. The picture Steinbeck painted of the land through which he traveled was not always pretty or encouraging, but he appeared to be telling things as he saw them. By 1960 many Americans were fed up with the lies of the Nixon/McCarthy cabal and the inadequate responses of those like Eisenhower, who were still trusted themselves. People were repelled by the behavior of those, like the Hawley son in *The Winter of Our Discontent*, who justified their behavior on the grounds that everybody was doing it.

Steinbeck probably would not have gone so far as the Beats in agreeing with Allen Ginsberg's startling accusation in the opening lines of *Howl*—"I saw the best minds of my generation destroyed by madness"—but he certainly longed for a different kind of society when he lamented that "American cities are like badger holes, ringed with trash" and then turned to praise the New England villages he visited as "the prettiest . . . in the whole nation, neat and white-painted, and [nearly] unchanged for a hundred years" (26–27)—a rural Arcadia. In one of the coolest reports on the new book, Eric F. Goldman in the *New York Times Book Review*, mouthpiece for all the elements in American society that Steinbeck most disapproved, observed. "This is a book about Steinbeck's America and for all the fascination of the volume, that America is hardly coincident with the United States in the Sixties."[5] But Steinbeck was giving literate Americans the kind of country that many of them had observed uneasily for themselves, while avoiding in this book overt political messages. The United States had become a place where, in the terms of Oscar Wilde's apothegm, the movers and shakers responsible for the society and the disciples ready and willing to prostitute themselves knew the price of everything and the value of nothing. Steinbeck could not really hope to conjure up any credible alternative to the wasteland he rediscovered but a nostalgic frontiersman's vision of what was past and passing in the dignified company of the great blue poodle.

Chapter Eleven

America and Americans

America and Americans is, as the presumptuous title intimates, Steinbeck's most important book for understanding the complex and sometimes contradictory man himself at a time when his creative career was over—though he had not yet admitted this—and he was nearing the end of his life. He wanted to put down here what he thought made his fellow Americans tick and what he liked and disliked about the ticking. The book is a long postscript to *Travels with Charley in Search of America*, although that is not what he had intended to write. What Steinbeck planned did not always work out; some things went awry, but there were some lucky accidents, and this was the last of them.

After finishing *Travels*, Steinbeck was at loose ends for a while, as nothing seemed to be shaping up. When he became depressed he tried to get back to retelling the King Arthur story, but when he found he couldn't get it going, he became even more depressed. After John F. Kennedy's shocking assassination, his widow asked Steinbeck if he would write a biography, but he did not feel up to the tremendous research that would be involved (Benson, 950). He did begin writing his own autobiography, but as Jackson Benson puts it, such plans "seemed to drift into limbo as he mulled them over in his mind, but never found solutions to the problems of form that they presented" (951).

Then, in August 1964, the new young head of Viking Press, Thomas H. Guinzburg, visited Steinbeck with a collection of photographs that he had commissioned to present a composite picture of the contemporary United States. At first, the plan had been to publish the book with only captions accompanying the works of prominent photographers, but Guinzburg got the idea that Steinbeck might like to write an introduction. The writer took on the project simply as a paying proposition, like much of his journalism, but he became absorbed in it, seeing a chance to talk about many matters he had wanted to bring up in *Travels* but had had to omit because of its narrative form. He did not want to use his experiences as springboards for a series of essays, a tendency he had succumbed to in *Sea of Cortez* and the overwrought chapter on Texans in *Travels*.

Work was disrupted by Pascal Covici's death and President Johnson's request for aid with his inaugural address, a Christmas trip to Ireland to visit John Huston, and the death of his sister Mary, so that he did not finish the job until October 1965. The book was not published until a year later, when it was presented in an imposingly large format for the Christmas gift trade. It was somewhat coolly received, however, as Steinbeck's close connections with President Johnson and his hawkish attitudes toward involvement in Vietnam had already alienated him from a majority of other writers and intellectuals, who strongly opposed Johnson's policies toward the conflict.

Steinbeck introduces the impressive volume as "in text and pictures . . . a book of opinions, unashamed and individual," attacking the "misconceptions and discourtesies" of evaluators who used the United States as "the natural patsy for those governments which were not doing so well." He goes on to say that he knew of "no native work of inspection of our whole nation and its citizens by a blowed-in-the-glass American." The feeling that the country has no parallel, he maintains, "has rarely been put down about our whole country" (Foreword, *America*, 7). (Robert DeMott in *Steinbeck's Reading* lists Henry Miller's *The Air-conditioned Nightmare* [1945] as one of the books Steinbeck owned or borrowed, but an expatriate diatribe like that or expatriate Henry James's elegantly selective *The American Scene* [1905] could hardly qualify.)

This is followed by nine essays illustrated with groups of relevant photographs (many in color), which may have suggested the essays but seem more likely to have been finally selected after the essays were completed, since only a few have direct connections with the text.

The opening essay, "E Pluribus Unum," stresses the assimilation into the new Western nation of a variety of European cultures and illustrates both the strengths and weaknesses of the method Steinbeck employs throughout. It also suggests the dubiousness of the choice of *America* as a synonym for the United States, especially in such a statement as "America did not exist four centuries ago" (13). Steinbeck makes some generalizations about the ways in which successive immigrant groups were absorbed into a mass culture and closes with some illustrative personal experiences, usually from his early years. In the first of these he reports that in the 1930s he had developed a new way of recognizing the states of origin of individual migrants. It ends with his surprise at a migrant's assertion that Steinbeck looked like a Californian, as he was not "aware that Californians had a look" (16). The essay wanders on to deal somewhat ill-advisedly with the two groups that had not been assimilated (although his discussion of African Americans is reserved for a later chapter).

While some politically incorrect labels date Steinbeck's essays, the more serious structural weakness here, as in many of the essays, is his concluding with generalized and often quite stereotyped discussions of trends and tendencies in "American" development, with quite unrepresentative examples drawn from his own experiences. Surely not all members of the groups he is discussing have the particular sensitivities of those whose conversations he recalls. He tends to equate the understanding of large groups with sympathetic encounters with unrepresentative individuals—a practice that works well in this first essay, but at times illustrates the problems in supporting generalizations with accounts of unique experiences. Although he stresses in his opening remarks that this is to be a book of individual opinions, he keeps forgetting that he is writing about *his* United States; and as he sagely observes in his essays on Paris, each individual has his or her own city or country. The better tone for a book such as this is one that shares unique experiences rather than universalizing one's own.

One cannot question a writer's methodologies if they serve the intended purpose, but one can point out that an individual mindset may clash with trying to suggest a consensus. The terminology used here dates the argument; identifying the principles from which it derives also establishes why the tide of sentiment was running against Steinbeck at the time he was writing. Already at that time another group was challenging the Anglo linguistic supremacy in California. What would Steinbeck have thought of a law that some thought necessary to establish English as the official language of the state? Mexicans were beginning to reclaim the lands they had earlier lost. Already a line of Spanish-language radio and TV stations were beginning to move beyond the border towns and establish themselves in the big northern cities.

From these somewhat dubious generalizations about the "American melting pot" (although Steinbeck does avoid that term), he moves on in "Paradox and Dream" to discuss the restless mobility of Americans (another trait of which he had a larger share than most) and to explore some of the paradoxes of American life, summing up our inconsistencies with the statement, "[S]ometimes we seem to be a nation of public puritans and private profligates" (30). Again he seems to be identifying his own complex personality with the general temper of the nation. Shaped by his growing up in a small town only one remove from the frontier, he knew little of life in the heavily populated, older, industrial communities.

He had apparently never pondered the implications of H. L. Mencken's possibly exaggerated pronouncement that the United States was the only nation that had ever gone from barbarism to decadence without an intervening period of civilization, possibly because his transition from his early years in semibarbarous California to his later years in decadent New York had not provided him with materials for speculating about a middle ground.

It is not surprising that he is particularly fascinated by the decadence of the trailer parks that had sprung up during his lifetime (here he reworks some material that he had already exploited in *Travels with Charley*). He seemed to think that the parks would become a greater presence in the culture, arguing that most of these "mobile homes" were in fact not moved but established on unpromising acreage near the edge of cities, where people could avoid municipal taxes. At the time of his travels with Charley, his roving home did attract the attention he expected; but only a decade later he would have found that with the interstate highway system developing, a new generation of travelers, even more restless than their predecessors, were no longer permanently parking their trailers or pulling them around with their automobiles or trucks. Following a model Steinbeck had pioneered, they had with the RV (recreation vehicle) incorporated the driver's seat into the cumbersome house itself, and hordes were moving incessantly or at least seasonally in pursuit of optimum living conditions, pulling their cars behind them. Home had become where you park it, and loyalty to locations was diminishing.

Steinbeck's origins and his tendency to revert back to them are also indicated by his question, "Who among us has not bought for a song an ancient junked car, and with parts from [others] put together something that could run?" (33). Even by 1965 the answer was not nearly so many of us as in the uncomplicated 1920s and impoverished 1930s, when such tinkering was portrayed affectionately in the popular comic strip "Gasoline Alley." The do-it-yourself movement certainly still flourishes, but in a computerized age it has taken on forms that Steinbeck could never have imagined just a few decades back. Again he seems to insist on identifying his personal world with the one around him, which was changing more rapidly and unpredictably than he probably enjoyed.

Evoking American dreams leads him into a discussion of "Government of the People," which largely reiterates stereotypes from the popular press about the rituals of American political life, especially election campaigns that avoid real issues. His statement, however, that one change brought about by the Depression was to make states' rights to a large extent anachronistic seems anachronistic itself. Just ahead, lay the presidential election in which a states' rights candidate (George Wallace) had the greatest influence in this century and brought into power the politician from Steinbeck's home state that he most distrusted.

Mention of the quarrels between federal and state governments over civil rights brings Steinbeck back around in "Created Equal" to the treatment of African Americans. Approaching this always touchy issue, he embraces a revisionist philosophy fashionable among midcentury historians stating flatly that slavery had not always been regarded as a sin and that "our present attitude toward slavery came into our thinking less than two hundred years ago" (57). Slavery, he goes on, had little to do with starting the Civil War, "except to give the differers an emotional platform" (60). As for abolitionists, he maintains that slavery would have been unprofitable in New England, and "it is easy to be uncompromisingly against the evil one does not need and cannot enjoy or profit by" (58).

He does not mention in his analysis of the problem that prevailing southern thought (with supporters elsewhere) held that African Americans were not "human beings" in the Anglo sense of the word but were products of a separate creation, and that even Lincoln himself—like Harriet Beecher Stowe—considered the only practicable solution to the "color" problem to be colonization, returning educated blacks to Africa to create a free, but definitely separate, society. Though Steinbeck believes African Americans will win their legal rights, he does not feel that true equality will be achieved until there is no vestige of suspicion between the races. Since he wrote, legal progress has been made, but tensions between racial groups—not just American blacks and whites— have intensified throughout the world.

Steinbeck again presents a problem by relying too much on personal examples. This time he dips back into the family past with tales of his paternal great-grandfather, who had gone to Palestine to Christianize the Jews by teaching them agriculture, and who, though strongly anti-slavery, used slaves without owning them by renting them from an Arab neighbor. (He does not mention at this point that most of the family was wiped out by an insurrection.) Then he introduces his great-aunt Carrie, who went South to open a school for Negro orphans. She was driven out by the Ku Klux Klan, but never surrendered her principles.

It is difficult to read either account as a success story. The exact point of the next chapter, "Genus Americanus," is even more elusive. From civil rights, Steinbeck moves appropriately to consideration of a classless society. It is soon clear that he is no more enthusiastic about classlessness than many of his contemporary writers and artists. He joins in a general chorus of midcentury complaints about the anonymous conformity of the corporation man and generally praises groups that deviate far from the norm, but finds his own examples among old-fashioned groups in small towns—not contemporary urban rebels. He praises the enjoyment in "grubby little towns" of the replacement of the formal orders and rituals of class-conscious societies with "unofficial orders, kingdoms, robes, and regalia and complicated forms of procedure and secret recognitions among the elect" (87). Finally, after denouncing literary censorship, with praise of "screwballs" as "charming, original and theatrical," though sometimes "malign, vicious . . . and downright dangerous" (89), he looks back to his childhood to tell about a local miser who starved his wife and daughter to death while hoarding $5,000 in gold that distant cousins found as they prepared to divide his land for building lots. The chapter ends with the curious statement that every community must have such eccentrics, but that "only when they hurt someone or die do we discover them" (92), a somewhat ghoulish perspective that seems an unlikely lead into a discussion of "The Pursuit of Happiness."

This essay turns into a particularly well illustrated reaction to American parenting and its influence on children, which concludes that what has been happening "doesn't work in that it does not create adults" but rather extends "adolescence far into the future, so that very many Americans have never and can never become adults" (93). Searching for a cause of a situation scarcely to be desired, he concludes that "we are living in two periods. Part of our existence has leaped ahead, and a part has lagged behind," so that "the young dread to grow up, the grown dread growing old, and the old are in a panic about sickness and uselessness" (105). Leisure, he feels, has become our new incurable disease; the only antidote he recommends is going back to the practice of small farmers of New England and the Midwest of creating the things that one uses oneself, as the already thriving do-it-yourself business was demonstrating.

Perhaps the aim of Steinbeck's judgments is apparent here. Despite the sweeping title of *America and Americans*, it is not a book for everyone. Rather, he is reenacting the joys and embarrassments, the community feeling and the bigotry of the society in which he grew up for the benefit of those from similar backgrounds, people who had exercised enormous influence, for better or worse, in shaping the pretechnological United States, but whose influence he was depressed to see waning as he wrote. It is an important book for understanding Steinbeck as an example of do-it-yourself-ism himself, as one who rose through his own efforts, shunning official channels as far as possible, to a position in which he was feted internationally.

We have reached the halfway point of the book as first published, but we have just about exhausted the text. The second half contains far fewer words than the first and a great many more unassimilated photographs. Those that are not really integrated into the discussion present—somewhat surprisingly in view of what we usually associate with Steinbeck—scenes from sports, the arts, and entertainment. It concludes with a stunning double-page spread of Carol Channing dancing the title number in *Hello, Dolly*, a period piece that brings to life the America that the book is actually about, and a great many local color shots that would be better suited to a richly illustrated edition of *Travels with Charley*.

There are three more short but important essays on Americans and the land, the world and the future. The first illustrates Steinbeck's undoubted commitments and shortcomings as an environmentalist. Denouncing the waste of resources, he again resorts to an illustration from his childhood to support his condemnation of the polluters that he thought could be shamed into doing right by the Victorian technique of moral suasion, although it has never proved widely successful in accomplishing anything but feuds. In "America and the World," he stresses that he thinks our time of insularity is over and ends with snatches from a conversation with an eminent unnamed American historian about how his knowledge of history, sociology, economics, and law might be strengthened—as Steinbeck's understanding of Russia had been—by a closer acquaintance with the great national literature.

A particularly interesting feature of this discussion since he did not often share such information, is the list of American novels that Steinbeck cites as enriching our knowledge of our culture. He mentions *The Adventures of Huckleberry Finn, An American Tragedy, Winesburg, Ohio, Main Street, The Great Gatsby, As I Lay Dying*—certainly a noteworthy list with which many might concur, but all novels by men active during his lifetime from Middle America, largely set in the postfrontier regions from which the characters come. All of them are about people who are trying—with varying success—to escape the scenes of their childhood, particularly young men (and one woman) seeking an identity for themselves, but none of whom find fulfillment in the long sought "territory" (as Huck Finn called it) beyond the horizon.

In "Americans and the Future," Steinbeck finally arrives at the conclusion toward which he has been inexorably moving. First he observes, as in his articles for *Le Figaro*, that he is not going to "preach about any good old days. By our standards of comfort they were pretty awful" (though he drew a lot of examples from them). But he does feel that one thing we have lost is the "rules" that they had "concerning life, limb and property, rules covering deportment, manners, conduct and rules defining dishonesty, dishonor, misconduct and crime." Although these rules were not always observed, violators were "savagely punished" (138). Now, however, he believes, "We have reached the end of a road and have no new path to take, no duty to carry out, and no purpose to fulfill." Although we have not discovered a new path, he confides, "I think we will find one, but its direction may be unthinkable to us now" (142).

Thus his personal quest ends in uncertainty. Roy Simmonds is right that *America and Americans* "is in some ways a deeply pessimistic work" that Steinbeck found painful to write.[1] His last major work is as open-ended as *The Grapes of Wrath*, as again he does not prescribe for readers but urges them to search for themselves. But what makes him think that a new path may be unthinkable at present? An answer may be that despite his putdown of the good old days, he did look backward toward what he perceived as a more ordered time, though its manner of living was no longer viable. He wished to recover the virtues of the past in a new setting; and he could not break out, any more than the characters in the novels he praises, from the mindset that we must keep pioneering to find some brave new world.

To understand his mindset, we might do well to look again at one of his favorite poems, Tennyson's dramatic monologue "Ulysses." The great Greek wanderer observes: "I cannot rest from travel, . . . all experience is an arch wherethro' / Gleams that untravell'd world, whose margin fades / For ever and for ever when I move." Steinbeck empathized with this vision that he projected into two of his greatest characters, Jody Tiflin and his grandfather in "The Red Pony," driven like Ulysses to be "Westering," traveling always through the arch of experience. Both are depressed by the workaday world of Jody's father, who works hard to maintain his ranch and does not dream of adventures. He is much like Ulysses' son Telemachus in the poem, of whom the father says, he willingly leaves his scepter, "to fulfill / This labour by slow prudence to make mild / A rugged people, and thro' soft degree / Subdue them to the useful and the good."

Perhaps the time has come when leaders must cease thinking of new worlds to conquer and devote themselves to subduing rugged people "to the useful and the good"—a process that can hardly be seen in operation in many parts of the world today. A "new way" may not be "unthinkable" at all, but not as exciting to think about as crossing new frontiers. Steinbeck had, as observed before, much of the popular figure the Lone Ranger about him, as many Americans do; but the time may have come to unmask and settle down to the difficult business of regenerating the wasteland.

America and Americans is finally just what Steinbeck promised it would be, "a book of opinions, unashamed and individual." It may not introduce readers to an always recognizable United States, but it certainly provides a unique introduction to John Steinbeck, a man whose accomplishments make him worth knowing as thoroughly as we can.

Chapter Twelve
"Letters to Alicia"

What turned out to be one of Steinbeck's longest, most controversial, most personally damaging, and least-known undertakings was launched unceremoniously on Saturday, 20 November 1965, in *Weekend with Newsday*, a supplement to the daily (except Sunday) newspaper for Long Island readers. Harry F. Guggenheim, who became the paper's editor after the death of his wife, Alice Patterson Guggenheim, who had founded the paper in 1940, announced its new contributor. John Steinbeck was leaving for Europe early in December on a long trip as a reporter who would send back weekly columns to the paper. These would be addressed to the late Mrs. Guggenheim, not, Steinbeck insisted, as a "mawkish or sentimental" gesture, but "to a living mind and a huge curiosity."[1] Still, the mortuary mode of the venture gave it that same air of discontent with the present—conjuring up the title of Steinbeck's last novel—and of longing for a better, vanished past that colored all of his writings of the 1960s.

As a practice run for this project—far more ambitious than those that he had tackled for the New York *Herald Tribune*, the Louisville *Courier Journal* syndicate, or Paris's *Le Figaro*, since the series would run for six months and then be renewed for another six in 1966–67—he launched forth on the prickly subject of government support for the arts, which was much in the news at the time as the National Foundation for the Arts had just been founded. Steinbeck was in a somewhat ambiguous position with regard to the subject, since he was suspicious of government control of the arts at the same time that he was a good friend of President Johnson and wished to support his actions. He took the line that he had disapproved of such programs because government support meant government intervention and censorship. Lately, however, his views had been shaken when Robert Lowell refused to attend President Johnson's Festival of the Arts because of his dismay over American foreign policy and when others lectured the president on their disapproval. The touchy president is reported to have said, "Some of them insulted me by staying away, and some of them insulted me by coming."[1] Steinbeck distanced himself from the event and his friend with the comment that Johnson probably never saw that the "battered and embattled White House is still in a state of siege," leading him to admit that he had been wrong about government involvement with the arts, "when the real danger lay in art getting into the government" (20 October 1965, 3W).

He continued to embroil himself in the increasing tension between the government and public opinion when he brought up the next week the "big dust-up" over the news that CBS-TV senior commentator Eric Sevareid had printed something that Adlai Stevenson had told him shortly before his death. Steinbeck refused to enter into the criticism of Sevareid, but observed that he hoped the commentator had considered whether Stevenson would have wanted the information (not disclosed in Steinbeck's column) released. By the third column, Steinbeck appeared hard pressed for ideas, as he used this opportunity to answer with acerbity a column that Max Lerner had written for the *New York Post* asking why Steinbeck had chosen to become a columnist. This gave him a chance to air his credentials by bringing up the *Figaro* pieces, to which little attention had been paid in the United States. He was quite unfashionably blunt and straightforward in saying, "When Harry Guggenheim offered to print and perhaps pay for the things I was going to do anyway, it seemed a very sweet idea." He acknowledged that writing columns, like painting pictures, might be the "dark working of an anthropophagic egomania," but he promised that "the moment these scatterings stop amusing me . . . I'll stop doing them" (4 December 1965, 3W). In the fourth column he continued this display of oneupmanship by confiding that he had been "an adviser to four Presidents—Mr. Roosevelt, Mr. Truman, Mr. Kennedy and Mr. Johnson," then modestly, but with less than candor, said he could "find no evidence that they ever took any of it" (11 November 1965, 3W).

Throughout these four trial runs from his home in Sag Harbor, Steinbeck appears to have been trying to establish an image of authority with a touch of diffidence to ward off insinuations that he might be taking himself too seriously by wandering out of his field, but the attempt does not quite come off. The very device of frequently addressing a dead woman distances him from the reader, who comes to feel like an eavesdropper reading other people's mail. Steinbeck was never able to put himself completely at ease in direct exchange with American readers. He could never relax with them the way he had with the crowd at the Paris "Kermesse des Etoiles," where he could keep the conversation at a superficially friendly level, partly because of his limited French, with a long queue that seemed unreservedly friendly. Because of the mixed reception to his work, ranging from laudation to condemnation, he never knew just where he stood with the American public. His uneven success as an autobiographer resulted in large measure from his trying to determine how much of himself he could reveal without revealing too much—a problem that never bothered Norman Mailer or Robert Lowell or others who made a profession of confession.

These early columns, aimed principally at treating quite serious matters amusingly, are interesting as his attempt late in life to work out an approach to an unfamiliar assignment. In his earlier reports from the European war zone and Russia and elsewhere, the setting provided the subject; but now he had to come up with his own until he became, like our troops, bogged down in Vietnam.

These "Letters to Alicia" have never been collected. There are many possible reasons why, but one is that many of them are of too ephemeral interest, either at the time they were written or afterward. The reports from abroad started unpropitiously, not with something about London as Steinbeck found it preparing for Christmas but with the first column to be devoted to Vietnam. Steinbeck questioned the confidence that could be put in the statements of two soldiers released by the Viet Cong as a gesture of goodwill and dismissed those like them who were protesting the U.S. involvement in the conflict by countering the statements of the soldiers with his own: "Well, we do belong there and we never wanted to win. But I believe we intend to make sure that Peking doesn't win, either" (18 December 1965, 3W). (Throughout the two years he was writing these columns, he held China responsible for supporting the Viet Cong, despite the long hostilities between the Chinese and Vietnamese and the evidence that the guerillas were receiving their principal support from Russia.)

He tried to restore a jolly tone to the columns by next reviving an idea that he had broached earlier about adding to the president's cabinet a Secretary of Nonsense; but in this Christmas Day publication he could not avoid turning the subject back to Vietnam to observe that he felt sure President Johnson "wants to get out of Vietnam more than anyone else," while at the same time venting his anger at the Department of State's refusing to grant him permission to visit China because it couldn't protect them there. The reply he shared with the public was, "Hell! You can't even protect me in Central Park" (25 December 1965).

His attention shifted from Vietnam because of personal problems. His next two columns involve an arcane misunderstanding with an old friend, Professor Eugene Vinaver, probably the foremost Malory scholar, about the nature of some manuscripts they had perused in Great Britain. Most readers appear to have been left confused by the whole matter, and Steinbeck stopped trying to straighten out the record and took off for County Kerry, at the extreme southwestern tip of Ireland, the westernmost point in Europe, where he and his wife Elaine spent Christmas with film director John Huston. From here he submitted reports about the difficulties of playing Father Christmas and a troublesome ghost in the neighborhood.

Steinbeck was getting tired and wanted to go home, but Harry Guggenheim prevailed on him to make his first visit to Israel before returning to Long Island. The Steinbecks arrived there in early February, just about the time of his sixty-fourth birthday; but the first letter from Tel Aviv did not appear until 26 February. Meanwhile, although Steinbeck had sent one from London that told about his paternal great-grandfather's family, which he had previously written about in *America and Americans*. His great-grandfather had moved to Palestine before the Civil War to try to Christianize the Jews only to have his model farm destroyed and his brother killed by wandering Bedouins. The great-grandfather escaped with his wife to the American consulate in Jaffa, and on the trip home his daughter was so badly mauled by the crew that she died after reaching port—hardly memories to generate a great affection for the region, especially when a search for his Uncle Charley's grave proved unsuccessful.

A much longer column published on 28 February is the most bizarre piece in the series, an example of a malevolent sense of humor that occasionally breaks through in some of Steinbeck's work, such as *Cannery Row* and his later short stories. The column consists of a reprinting of an account by Ephraim Kishon, a reporter for the Jerusalem *Post*, of a conversation that he overheard in a restaurant where Steinbeck was trying to get breakfast. The writer is confronted by an overbearing waiter who calls him Mr. Steinberg and insists on relating his life story instead of taking Steinbeck's order.

To this Steinbeck appends a copy of a letter that he addressed to the editor of the *Post*, explaining that several of his friends found Kishon's column funny, but that "it isn't funny and it is not intended to be" (28 February 1966, 3W). Then he goes on with a fantastic tale about this waiter whom he calls Zorba becoming his secretary and becoming so attached to Steinbeck that the writer fears he will stow away on his plane back to the United States. Once again, as in the Paris series, Steinbeck cannot resist his propensity for fictionalizing his reporting.

The fun quickly disappears, for in his next column he uses the Israeli youths' sense of patriotic service to lash out at America's "balding youth," burning draft cards to protest our continued entanglement in Vietnam: "It wasn't all protest against the inconvenience of living in a world they never made," he rages. "Hell, they never made anything. There were other ways to live hopelessly." He specifically mentions surfing, rioting on the beaches, and sitting hypnotized by folk songs. He ends up with one of his few comments about the Beats, who "had it worked out that Sartre and Camus and selected synthesized eastern philosophies forbade effort of any kind, including washing" (5 March 1966, 3W).

His tone becomes increasingly cranky when he visits an Israeli bookstore and finds there a copy of one of his books printed in English in Moscow. He breaks his resolution about criticizing the Russians only to their faces because he has discovered that "they not only steal my books [they pay no royalties] but distribute them in non-Communist countries, and this is dirty, stinking, chicken-dirt petty larceny" (26 March 1966, 3 W). This complaint is certainly justified, but it indicates an increasingly irritable and depressed state of mind as he tries to get in touch with the contemporary world—a state of mind that leads him, in his last two columns about Israel, to return to the past. He tells the heroic but tragic story of the doomed defense of Masada by a small remnant of Jews making a last stand against the overpowering Roman forces in ancient times.

His columns did not end with his travels, for he continues through to the end of May with further reports from Sag Harbor. On 30 April he returns to one of the matters that had troubled him during his travels with Charley and wonders whether Congress has at last passed a beautification law promoted by Lady Bird Johnson. (An ironic sidelight on this effort is that the last set of postage stamps authorized by the Johnson administration called attention to the extensive floral plantings that the first lady had prompted in the national capital to further this cause. When Nixon came into office, these colorful tributes to one affirmative American impulse were withdrawn from sale.) Steinbeck recalls that he had written that the United States seemed to be becoming one vast junkyard and concludes that we probably cannot eliminate all the junk but at least we might mask it by plantings flowers and trees. Still, he suspects such improvements cannot be achieved by ordinance but only by a sense of neighborly cooperation—an indication that by this time he had little faith in a fundamental change taking place and would be content to mask the decay.

Despite this underlying sense of defeat, he fought on like the pathetic band at Masada. He had previously resisted going to Vietnam, but when his son John was sent there by the army, he decided that the time had come. President Johnson had asked him to go over as his private envoy to report on conditions, but Steinbeck did not want to serve as an agent even for a friend whom he admired. He agreed to make a trip again as a correspondent for *Newsday;* but he did not tell the president in advance that he was going, and he insisted that Elaine accompany him, as he was getting too old to go off for any length of time by himself. He had also tried to work out a visit with the Russian poet Yevgeny Yevtushenko to both South and North Korea, but the Russian had to beg off, probably under government pressure. (It is not clear that the American administration would have greeted this idea with any great enthusiasm, either.)

He left in December 1966 and eventually visited Laos, Thailand, Indonesia, Hong Kong, and Japan, as well as South Korea; but he was never able to get into China, Cambodia, or North Korea. There are thirty-three columns in this series, beginning 10 December 1966 from Sag Harbor, after a notice of the new series on 3 December. The first letter from Saigon appears just before Christmas on 24 December. Beginning 19 January, while he was in the war zone, two columns a week usually appeared until the end of March. The last one sent from Saigon was printed 20 February 1967. The next five came from Thailand. Then he moved on to Laos and Bali and sent three final columns from Japan. This time there were no follow-ups at home.

The three warm-up columns he wrote are considerably more mellow than those of the first series. Steinbeck appears more sure of his audience, of the scope of his assignment, of his own aims. When he first writes from Saigon, he is still in a playful mood befitting the holiday season, satirizing the packages that well-meaning families and friends send to the war zones by recommending all the wrong approaches.

Serious business begins with the last column published in 1966, on New Year's Eve, as Steinbeck reports the difficulties of landing safely in Saigon. He praises a new village that the Vietnamese have built for themselves with contributions collected in Gadsden, Alabama, to replace those from which the Viet Cong drove them after killing all the men; and he gets in some swipes at Senators Fulbright (Arkansas) and Wayne Morse (Oregon), leading liberals who were not embracing President Johnson's policies.

With the new year and Steinbeck's trips to the battle zone, a problem of the literary critic's role arises, for the string of reports over the next two months are neither very interesting reading nor interesting to read about.[2] What becomes clear is that, although Steinbeck was there only as a reporter, or perhaps because he was a reporter, plans for his visit were worked out very carefully. He was seeing what the military wanted him to see, since he was an influential friend who might help improve the image of U.S. participation at a time when critics were more numerous than collaborators at home. (Unfortunately, *Newsday* was not likely to win new friends or influence people. It was a suburban paper directed to a generally cautious audience of middle-class commuters who constituted the limited support the administration could call upon.) By 1967, young persons of draft age had practically consolidated against American participation in an internal struggle in a remote area of the world with a long history of factional warfare.

Steinbeck's columns come faster than before, but they have less sense of direction. The reports become as shapeless and aimless as the shifting zones of hostile activity. While Steinbeck claims that his reports from Saigon are only self-censored, they conspicuously lack extended discussion of the ideological aspects of the conflict. Once away from the battle, his attacks on the Viet Cong become strident again, suggesting that old hands on the scene may have tried his own policy of neighborly pressure on him, not to suppress his comments but to intimate the benefits of following a more circumspect line while he was in the line of fire himself. Only specialists interested in reconstructing battlefield tactics would find much interest in these reports, and Vietnam does not seem to have appealed to many such armchair strategists.

With his first column from Bangkok (25 February 1967), Steinbeck begins hurling invective again when he answers charges that American forces were bombing civilian areas in Hanoi. This had been testified to by two reputable American reporters, with a suspicion aroused by his examining photographs that the buildings in question had not been bombed from the air, but from the ground, as such destruction "would be a small price to pay for propaganda to change and harden world opinion" against the United States (3W).

The last report from Saigon (20 February—it had evidently been delayed in delivery, for it reports that the Steinbecks are preparing to leave for Bangkok) is one of the few memorable ones in the group that can serve as an example of Steinbeck's talents as a reporter. One gets a feeling that the change of scene has freed him from some kind of hypnotic enchantment that being physically involved in the action had cast over him. He is recalling the final mission he flew in Vietnam in an ancient plane called Puff, the Magic Dragon. He admits that he has been in dangerous situations during the past five weeks, but becomes scared that an accidental shot might hit this flare-laden plane and blow it up. "I was scared," he confesses, "I thought how silly it would be on my last night. I think it was the first time I had thought of myself, me, as being in danger" (3W). This extreme personal reaction brings back to his mind the valued friends that he had lost, Ernie Pyle and Robert Capa, the photographer who had been killed as he was preparing to leave for Paris after his last assignment in Vietnam. Free of any propagandistic overtones, the report captures a man's sudden blinding revelation of his vulnerability. It also brings back to the reader that what one seeks to find in Steinbeck's reports is not the elusive reality about why we were in Vietnam but something of Steinbeck himself as he suddenly discovers himself as a man who is there.

Chapter Thirteen
A Legacy in Disarray

Can one speak of John Steinbeck's "career" as a nonfiction writer? "Career" suggests a period of steady, coherent activity, even if one makes a late start. One can discuss Steinbeck's career as a fiction writer even if he made a somewhat late start after a failed first attempt to become a journalist and retired somewhat early to spend his last years primarily on autobiographical material. He produced long and short novels and short stories consistently and sometimes with surprising rapidity for more than thirty years.

What we have been examining in this book is the product of a number of starts—often inspired starts—also over a period of thirty years, which often led to sudden and disappointing conclusions. During these episodes, he produced eleven works of sufficient size and scope to be comparable with his twenty fiction works—more of both than many other noted writers. Only three of these nonfiction works were written for immediate publication as books—*Sea of Cortez* (1941), *Travels with Charley in Search of America* (1962), and *America and Americans* (1966). Five were originally written as a series of newspaper articles and then published in book form, often revised, sometimes relatively shortly afterward—"The Harvest Gypsies" (1936) as *Their Blood Is Strong* (1938), *A Russian Journal* (1947, 1948), *Un Américain à New York et à Paris* (1954, 1956, in French only)—one years later—*Once There Was a War* (1943, 1959). The "Letters to Alicia" have not been collected and probably never will be because of their unevenness and the seriously dated nature of some. The other three, most self-revealing portraits of the artist at work, were not written with publication in mind and appeared only posthumously: *Working Days* (1938, 1989), *Journal of a Novel: The "East of Eden" Letters* (1951, 1969), *Zapata: A Narrative in Dramatic Form of the Life of Emiliano Zapata* (1949, 1991). All were connected with major fictional works in progress.

"The Harvest Gypsies" and *Working Days* were related to the evolution of the *The Grapes of Wrath* and were never considered by Steinbeck as steps toward a new career. He plunged into *Sea of Cortez* with great enthusiasm, contemplating a career as a marine biologist; but he became impatient with the book and cut it short. He also cut short the trip to the Mediterranean Theater in World War II and for years did nothing about the reports finally collected in *Once There Was a War.* Domestic problems precluded following up *A Russian Journal* with similar work. He was apparently not connected with the book publication of *Un Américain*, and, although he wrote a number of other short journalistic pieces during the mid-1950s, he made no effort to collect them. Even his travels with Charley were cut short, and he contemplated no more such journey. *America and Americans* he apparently considered as an end itself, the chance to express his feelings about the United States. Whether he at first considered the "Letters to Alicia" anything more than a chance to make money for further traveling, we shall never know, because to an undeniable extent the exhausting junket to Eastern Asia did him in. Had he survived and his health permitted, there is no reason to suppose he might not have continued his traveling and reporting, with book publication not necessarily in mind.

Since Steinbeck's death in 1968, his fiction has fared better than his nonfiction, though readers and scholars can well be grateful for the posthumous publication of the journals written with *The Grapes of Wrath* and *East of Eden.* Both Steinbeck's American and English publishers are bringing out new "classic" editions of his works. Even more important from scholars' and collectors' viewpoints, the highly selective Library of America has begun to add to its seventy-one volumes, covering the whole range of the national literature, a multivolume set of Steinbeck's works, arranged chronologically. In all these commendable projects, however, the emphasis will understandably be on his widely read fiction. It is unlikely that any material that has not already appeared in book form will be included, although more diaries may turn up, such as the one kept in 1946 while he was writing *The Wayward Bus.*[1]

This entry of Steinbeck's work into projects to establish a permanent record of the best American writing raises, of course, the problem of the permanent value of the nonfiction. Opinions in such a matter can only be like Steinbeck's own in *America and Americans;* but already it is possible to make some disinterested judgments about probable permanent interest in the subjects and a "dated" quality of any of the writings.

Again, the two journals cited above are most likely to remain of interest as long as the novels continue to hold readers' interest. "The Harvest Gypsies" essays, on the other hand, have been in and out of print several times already. Many people probably feel that these early reports about the migrants have been largely assimilated into *The Grapes of Wrath* and the more general history of the Depression. *Zapata* would also seem to face an uncertain future, unless the people of the United States in the future develop closer ties with their southern neighbors that lead to greater interest in Mexican fiction. Both *Once There Was a War* and *A Russian Journal* will continue to find audiences as these highly personal accounts of two vitally important episodes in American history throw light on these increasingly remote times. It would be valuable to have a newly edited, combined collection of the full reports. Two of Steinbeck's most personal works, the log from *Sea of Cortez* and *Travels with Charley*, are among those that have been most discussed by literary critics. There should always be a market for them as long there is interest in the personality of the artist himself. All four of the books just mentioned are uneven in quality, but readers need to consider them in their totality to get a fair impression.

More difficult problems are posed by the works that have already been neglected, especially since they are highly opinionated accounts that have not pleased some readers and that often present the author's speculations more than his experiences. This is true of the "Letters to Alicia." *America and Americans* is something vastly more important, a final statement of Steinbeck's credo after an extensive examination of himself and his relation to his nation and its people. While many of the pictures that sparked the book are most impressive, they are not indispensable to Steinbeck's argument. In fact, many of them are not closely related to the text. For those wishing to become deeply acquainted with Steinbeck's thoughts and feelings to the extent that he has made them public only in this book, the ornaments are distracting. The book is invaluable in developing an understanding of the writer; but it is not possible to guess how many people really want to become that well acquainted with the man, who in the period of his greatest work insisted that he wanted to be known only through that fiction. The prevailingly old-fashioned tone of Steinbeck's judgments are not likely to attract many disciples.

The greatest necessity, however, in presenting enough of the rare autobiographical material to the public to facilitate an understanding of the writer at a period of one of his important self-revaluations is a first publication of the original English texts for the pieces published in *Le Figaro* in 1954, as Steinbeck wrote them. All of these are extant; but four of them are not known to have been published in English, and subsequent English-language versions of others differ from the French. What is needed is *not* a rendition of the text of the Paris book in English, particularly since it contains some totally unrelated pieces from other sources and rearranges the order of the appearance of the columns in the Paris paper, but an edition from the English manuscripts of the seventeen "pieces" that Steinbeck wrote for *Le Figaro*, in the order of their composition, with comments on any significant variations of the French translations from Steinbeck's originals.

These "pieces" are important, because even though they are uneven in interest and significance and even style, the best of them present, in a way that nothing else in Steinbeck's writing does, a picture of the writer undergoing a process of self-discovery. There are no similar accounts of such a sea change during such a concentrated period, except the two journals that he kept while writing *The Grapes of Wrath* and *East of Eden*; and these were not intended for general audiences. The reports from *Sea of Cortez* to *Travels with Charley* were written after Steinbeck had had time to reconsider his experiences selectively. It is only the *Figaro* pieces that record a sustained spontaneity of response, culminating—following reporter Maria Crapeau's question about American writers dwelling on the past and Steinbeck's recognition of its application to his own recent work—with his later lyrical response that "No Paris I can see is the real Paris except to me. I must learn to be sure of this. . . . I must get a little Paris of my own and defend it against all others as the real Paris" ("Reality," 376).

Here "Lone Ranger" Steinbeck comes unabashedly in control as he realizes that each individual's perceptions are isolated experiences. The "community" Arthur Miller saw Steinbeck as seeking, where he could be more than an observer and commentator, did not exist. There was no universal experience and indeed there was "no big soul ever'body's a part of," as Jim Casy envisions in *The Grapes of Wrath* (33), except in the sense of accepting others and their private worlds as being as valid as one's own.

It was this acceptance of the uniqueness of his personal vision that carried Steinbeck through his two final novels. Pippin IV prepares to give up for good his position in Paris and his overwhelming responsibility for decisions that the people did not really want him to make. Ethan Allen Hawley realizes in *The Winter of Our Discontent* that his responsibility is not to a corrupted wasteland community but to his daughter, to whom he must return the family talisman, "lest another light go out."

These are not Steinbeck's most effective novels, and he did not devote the rest of his life to this isolated vision; but it supported him through what proved one of the happiest periods of his personal life until he sallied forth to rediscover his country and found it in need of following a new path that it had not found. The *Figaro* papers chart Steinbeck's course as he begins to find a new way of his own, and they need to be read in the context of his day-to-day thoughts as he gropes for a path toward a sense of personal peace from 1954 to 1960, when in the course of his travels to rediscover the United States, as T. S. Eliot puts it at the end of "The Love Song of J. Alfred Prufrock," human voices wake him and he drowns.

Toward Autobiography

Beyond proper preservation of the *Figaro* papers, a larger project looms. While Steinbeck did not write an autobiography, he left behind a large body of nonfiction writing, including a number of occasional pieces too numerous and scattered to examine in this survey of the highlights of this part of his career. Together these constitute a kind of daybook of reminiscences from years back and a few moments ago that provide a sketchy, sporadic, but stimulating account of his life. There could be compiled from these a leisurely volume that would offer readers a chance to discover the man for themselves. I hope that one will soon become available to join his already published letters in offering a rounded picture of how he communicated with both his intimates and the larger community during the changing phases of his life.

One problem that such a book would have to contend with is what finally happened during the 1960s to shatter the sense of immediacy that Steinbeck had cultivated in Paris and drove him back into the more contemplative moralism that he talked of seeking in the *East of Eden* journal. Part of the answer, as already suggested, lies in the shocks he received from immediate involvement with certain aspects of American culture, especially the New Orleans Cheerleaders, as recorded in *Travels with Charley.* This gave him back a sense of "lostness" that he communicates in *America and Americans.*

We must also, however, consider the deleterious features of the great honor of being awarded the Nobel Prize for literature. Steinbeck had always been justifiably suspicious of such honors and had rejected those from lesser sources, but finally even he succumbed to the call from Stockholm.

After questioning in his acceptance speech whether he deserved this honor over other contenders and acknowledging his pride and pleasure at receiving it, he turned to "the high duties and responsibilities of the makers of literature"—a heavy burden that this aging Lone Ranger felt the community had imposed upon him. After knocking "a pale and emasculated critical priesthood singing their litanies in empty churches," he acknowledges that "[h]umanity has been passing through a gray and desolate time of confusion" and argues that the writer is "charged with exposing our many grievous faults and failures . . . for the purpose of improvement."[2] The text is full of noble sentiments, but one stops short to contemplate the implications of that word "improvement," which carries us back to the nineteenth-century concept of "improving each shining hour" and the world that Steinbeck would conjure up in *America and Americans.* He felt that he must not, like Ethan Allen Hawley in his last novel, accept a lonely charge to keep one small candle burning but must accept the burden thrust on him by the agents of community to function, as his son John IV describes him in *In Touch* (1969), "a kind of American conscience figure."[3]

Can anyone play such a role convincingly? One needs to recall that Steinbeck, after risking a dangerous junket to Vietnam that made him more foes than friends, finally injured himself in what was to prove a disastrous way, trying to lend a helping hand.[4]

Ending on a Personal Note

The question that I am most often asked about Steinbeck—and that not frequently—is whether I ever met him. The answer is no. I have met his wife Elaine, who is a charming, exciting person, brimming over with the Texas vigor that led me to do my graduate work in that dynamic state after the Army had accidentally introduced us during World War II. I also subsequently greatly enjoyed working with Steinbeck's editor Pascal Covici on *A Companion to "The Grapes of Wrath."* I have, however, located one comment that Steinbeck made about me—as a universal type really rather than an individual. Because this book winds up a long professional association with his work, I thought it should be put on record.

On 6 November 1961, with my first Twayne series book about Steinbeck in circulation since June, Covici wrote to the novelist that he had received a copy and for the first time had been able to read a book about him without cringing.[5] Steinbeck replied from Paris on 10 November that he would be amused to read what a Florida professor had to say about him, but in response to Covici's comments about my "understanding" his work, he queried, "but what?" He goes on to say that Alfred Kazin and others who were sorry he was not Kafka understood, too. (My point had been that I was pleased to find his work was at that time unfashionably like Kafka's and that it should be appreciated on its own merits.)

My understanding of Steinbeck's work has always been based on trying to read it in the light of the comment that he made to his agents and publisher when he decided to destroy the novel called "L'Affaire Lettuceberg": "My whole work drive has been aimed at making people understand each other" (*Working Days*, xl). I hope I understood Steinbeck to some extent.

I bring this matter up not to exploit one glancing connection with John Steinbeck but to raise a question fundamental to further understanding of the man and his work—how much did he want to be understood? One side of his multifaceted personality took delight in the secret quality in his work. Very early in his career, he wrote to a friend of *To A God Unknown*, "From a novel about people, it has become a novel about the world. And you must never tell it. It must be found out. . . . It will be confused, analyzed, analogized, criticised, and none of our fine critics will know what is happening" (Benson, 260). This tendency did not disappear with success and fame. On 3 December 1944, after advance copies of *Cannery Row* had been sent out for review, Steinbeck wrote to Covici, "There is a time in every writer's career when the critics are gunning for him to whittle him down"; then, after the novel appeared, he wrote in January, "It is interesting to me, Pat, the reason for these little chapters in C. R. . . . Nearly all lay readers know. Only critics don't."[6]

Steinbeck has often been reviewed and criticized most unfairly and uncomprehendingly, but he seems to hope that the critics will be wrong, so that his faith in ordinary readers will be vindicated. What he seemed to have hoped for most of all in aiming to make people understand each other was being understood by his readers without critical intervention as members of an intimate group. There was something of the small Victorian town lodge rituals that he speaks of in *America and Americans* (87), with their titles and secrets those like of the knights of King Arthur's Round Table, that shaped his sense of community. The critics were the outsiders—like the wolves howling for the vice-principal in one of his short stories—seeking to destroy the comradeship of good fellows. How much this tendency that was the fancy dress escape of the lodge members from the rigorous job of building a nation during the years of great expansion has led to initiates' understanding and outsiders' misunderstanding of Steinbeck's coded messages is beyond assessment. But it certainly must be kept in mind, especially when confronting inconsistencies in his attitudes. He did have a tendency toward the metaphysical, especially in its gaudier manifestations, which colored his fiction more than his reporting, but which did lead him away from addressing tough events to allegorizing. Let us ride into the sunset with the Lone Ranger image that I have been belaboring, contemplating that John Steinbeck's fictions were his many masks and speculating how much he unmasked in his nonfiction.

Notes and References

Preface

1. Jackson J. Benson, *The True Adventures of John Steinbeck, Writer* (New York: Viking, 1984), 702; hereafter cited in the text as Benson. Biographical information not identified as from other sources has been checked against this book.

Chapter One

1. John Steinbeck, "Autobiography: Making of a New Yorker," *New York Times Magazine,* 1 February 1953, 26–27.
2. For an account of the writing of the novel, see John Steinbeck, *Working Days: The Journals of "The Grapes of Wrath,"* ed. Robert DeMott (New York: Viking, 1989); hereafter cited in the text as *Working Days.*
3. Peter Lisca, *The Wide World of John Steinbeck* (New Brunswick, N.J.: Rutgers University Press, 1958), 197; hereafter cited in the text as Lisca.
4. Elaine Steinbeck and Robert Wallsten, eds., *Steinbeck: A Life in Letters* (New York: Viking, 1975) 265; hereafter cited in the text as *Life in Letters.*
5. John Steinbeck, *America and Americans* (New York: Viking, 1966), 127; hereafter cited in the text as *America.*
6. Jay Parini, *John Steinbeck: A Biography* (London: Heinemann, 1994), 312; hereafter cited in the text as Parini.
7. Elaine Steinbeck tells the story of their choice in an interview with Donald V. Coers, published in *After "The Grapes of Wrath": Essays on John Steinbeck in Honor of Tetsumaro Hayashi*, ed. Coers et al. (Athens: Ohio University Press, 1994), 241–71; hereafter cited in the text as Coers et al.
8. John Steinbeck, *Travels with Charley in Search of America* (New York: Viking, 1962), 6; hereafter cited in the text as *Travels.*

Chapter Two

1. John Steinbeck, "Dubious Battle in California," *Nation,* 13 September 1936, 304.
2. John Steinbeck, *Cup of Gold* (New York: Robert M. McBride, 1929), 255.
3. Warren French, ed., *A Companion to "The Grapes of Wrath"* (New York: Viking, 1963), 54; subsequent page references in the text are cited from John Steinbeck, *Their Blood Is Strong* (San Francisco: Simon J. Lubin Society of California, 1938), in which the newspaper columns were reprinted with an "Epilogue," as this pamphlet is reprinted in the collection hereafter cited in the text.

Chapter Three

1. Background information about this trip is provided by contributions to the *"Cannery Row* Fiftieth Aniversary Edition" of the *Steinbeck Newsletter,* Fall 1995.

2. John Steinbeck, *The Log from "Sea of Cortez"* (New York: Viking, 1951), 237; hereafter cited in the text as *The Log.* This paperbound reprinting does not contain the colored plates from *Sea of Cortez,* but it is the only book to contain "About Ed Ricketts."

3. Sparky Enea (as told to Audry Lynch), *With Steinbeck in the Sea of Cortez* (Los Osos, Calif.: Sand River Press, 1991), is a gossipy account of life aboard the *Western Flyer* during the expedition by the radio operator.

4. Richard Astro, *John Steinbeck and Edward F. Ricketts: The Shaping of a Novelist* (Minneapolis: University of Minnesota Press, 1973), 26–42, contains the fullest account of Ricketts's influence on Steinbeck, but it should be read in conjunction with Benson's later biography, 479–82.

5. J. D. Salinger, "Seymour: An Introduction," in *"Raise High the Roof Beam, Carpenters" and "Seymour: An Introduction"* (Boston: Little, Brown, 1963), 124; hereafter cited in the text as Salinger.

6. John Steinbeck, *Cannery Row* (New York: Viking, 1945), 23; *The Log,* xxxix.

Chapter Four

1. Renata Berg-Pan, *Leni Riefenstahl* (Boston: Twayne, 1980), 147.

2. Donald V. Coers, *John Steinbeck as Propagandist: "The Moon Is Down" Goes to War* (Tuscaloosa: University of Alabama Press, 1991), discusses the reception of the novel in occupied countries.

3. Clifford Lewis, "Steinbeck: The Artist as FDR Speech-Writer," in *Rediscovering Steinbeck: Revisionist Views of His Art, Politics, and Intellect,* ed. Cliff Lewis and Carrol Britch (New York: Edwin Mellem Press, 1989), 195.

4. Clifford Lewis, "Art for Politics," in *After "The Grapes of Wrath,"* ed. Coers et al., 24.

5. John Steinbeck, foreword to *Speeches of Adlai Stevenson* (New York: Random House, 1957), 6–7.

Chapter Five

1. John Steinbeck, *Once There Was a War* (New York: Viking, 1958), vi; hereafter cited in the text as *War.*

2. Kurt Vonnegut, *Breakfast of Champions* (New York: Delacorte Press/Seymour Lawrence, 1973), 181.

3. Roy Simmonds tells more of the story of Big Train Mulligan in *John Steinbeck: The War Years, 1939–1945* (Lewisburg, Pa.: Bucknell University Press, 1995).

Chapter Six

1. John Steinbeck, *A Russian Journal* (New York: Viking, 1948), 4; hereafter cited in the text as *Russian Journal*.

Chapter Seven

1. John Steinbeck, *Zapata,* ed. Robert E. Morsberger (New York: Penguin, 1993), 16; hereafter cited in the text as *Zapata*.
2. See Joseph R. Millichap, *Steinbeck and Film* (New York: Ungar, 1983), 121–23, and Thomas H. Pauly, *An American Odyssey* (Philadelphia: Temple University Press, 1983), 145–51, for accounts of the difficulties that Steinbeck and Elia Kazan experienced trying to bring *Viva Zapata!* to the screen.
3. Elia Kazan, *Elia Kazan: A Life* (New York: Knopf, 1988), 397–401.

Chapter Eight

1. John Steinbeck, *Journal of a Novel: The "East of Eden" Letters* (New York: Viking, 1969), 98; hereafter cited in the text as *"Eden" Letters*.
2. The manuscript is located with other valuable Steinbeck papers, including the originals of the *Le Figaro* "pieces," in the Harry Ransom Humanities Research Center at the University of Texas–Austin.
3. This admission about wanting to get away from a sense of immediacy in his postwar fiction sheds light on his response to a question raised in Paris in 1954 by interviewer Maria Crapeau about American writers' obsession with the past. This will be discussed in chapter 9.
4. Warren French, *John Steinbeck's Fiction Revisited* (New York: Twayne, 1994), 118.
5. Wayne C. Booth, *The Rhetoric of Fiction* (Chicago: University of Chicago Press, 1961), 8.

Chapter Nine

1. The seventeen "pieces" in the order that Steinbeck wrote and numbered them (undated) are described in the entry for *Le Figaro* in Brian Railsback, ed., *The John Steinbeck Encyclopedia* (Westport, Conn.: Greenwood, 1996).
2. John Steinbeck, *Un Américain à New-York et à Paris,* trans. Jean-François Rozan (Paris: René Julliard, 1956, 71–77; hereafter cited in the text as *Paris*. The English text of this passage is from "Fishing in Paris," *Punch,* 25 August 1954, 248–49. When not otherwise specified in the text, translations are by the author.
3. English text from "Capital Roundup—with John Steinbeck in Paris," *Saturday Review,* 16 April 1955, 8.
4. John Steinbeck, "Trust Your Luck," *Saturday Review,* 13 January 1957, 44.

    5.   John Steinbeck, "A Plea for Tourists," *Punch,* 26 January 1955, 148.
    6.   John Steinbeck, "The Yank in Europe," *Holiday,* January 1956, 25.
    7.   John Steinbeck, "Cooks of Wrath," *Everybody's,* 9 April 1955, 15.
    8.   John Steinbeck, "Reality and Illusion," *Punch,* 17 November 1954, 616; hereafter cited in the text as "Reality."
    9.   Lawrence William Jones, "Random Thoughts from Paris," *Steinbeck Quarterly* 3 (Spring 1970): 29. Jones's brief comments were the first to inform Americans about the book. He was not aware of the appearance of the "pieces" in *Le Figaro.*
    10.   John Steinbeck, "Discovering the People of Paris," *Holiday,* August 1956, 36.
    11.   John Steinbeck, "Good Guy—Bad Guy," *Punch,* 22 September 1954, 376.

Chapter Ten

    1.   John Ditsky, "Steinbeck's *Travels with Charley,*" in *Steinbeck's Travel Literature: Essays in Criticism,* ed. Tetsumaro Hayashi (Muncie, Ind.: Steinbeck Society of America, 1980), 56–61.
    2.   Richard Astro, in "Travels with Steinbeck: The Laws of Thought and the Laws of Things," *Steinbeck's Travel Literature,* ed. Hayashi, 1–11.
    3.   Paul McCarthy, *John Steinbeck* (New York: Ungar, 1980), 135.
    4.   For an extended comparison of Steinbeck's fiction with Salinger's, see Warren French, "Steinbeck and J. D. Salinger," in *Steinbeck's Literary Dimension,* ed. Tetsumaro Hayashi (Metuchen, N. J.: Scarecrow Press, 1973).
    5.   Eric F. Goldman, review of *Travels with Charley, New York Times Book Review,* 26 July 1962, 5.

Chapter Eleven

    1.   Roy S. Simmonds, "'Our land . . . incredibly dear and beautiful': Steinbeck's *America and Americans,*" in *Steinbeck's Travel Literature,* ed. Hayashi, 26.

Chapter Twelve

    1.   John Steinbeck, "Letters to Alicia," *Newsday,* 20 November 1965, 3-W; dated page references to the "Letters" are hereafter cited in the text.
    2.   The most detailed analysis of Steinbeck's letters from Vietnam is made in Tetsumaro Hayashi, *John Steinbeck and the Vietnam War,* part 1 (Muncie, Ind.: Steinbeck Research Institute, 1989). No further parts have been published.

Chapter Thirteen

    1.   This and two other journals written during 1950–52 are part of the extensive John Steinbeck collection at the Pierpont Morgan Library in New

York City. See Robert Parks, "John Steinbeck in the Pierpont Morgan Library," *Steinbeck Newsletter,* Winter–Spring 1995, 19–21.

2. John Steinbeck, *Speech Accepting the Nobel Prize for Literature* (New York: Viking), 1962), 7–8.

3. John Steinbeck IV, *In Touch* (New York: Knopf, 1969), xii.

4. In his last "Letter to Alicia" (13 May 1967), Steinbeck explains how he slipped a disk in his back helping a porter in Hong Kong take a handtruck loaded with beer up a staircase. He comments wryly, "My good deed had drawn maximum penalty" (2). The incident led to a series of complications that ended in his death.

5. The letters are in the Harry Ransom Humanities Research center at the University of Texas–Austin.

6. Thomas Fensch, *Steinbeck and Covici: The Story of a Friendship* (Middlebury, Vt.: Paul Eriksson, 1979), 43.

Selected Bibliography

PRIMARY WORKS

Autobiographical Nonfiction: Books

America and Americans. New York: Viking, 1966.
Un Américain à New York et à Paris. Paris: Réne Julliard, 1956 (translated into French by Jean-François Rozan).
Journal of a Novel: The "East of Eden" Letters. New York: Viking, 1969.
The Log from "Sea of Cortez." New York: Viking, 1951 (also contains "About Ed Ricketts").
Once There Was a War. New York: Viking, 1959.
Positano. Salerno, Italy: Ente Provinciale per il Turismo, 1954; in Italian. English and French editions, 1959.
A Russian Journal. New York: Viking, 1948.
Sea of Cortez, with Edward F. Ricketts. New York: Viking, 1941.
Speech Accepting the Nobel Prize for Literature. New York: Viking, 1962.
Their Blood Is Strong. San Francisco: Simon J. Lubin Society of California, 1938.
Travels with Charley in Search of America. New York: Viking, 1962.
Working Days: The Journals of "The Grapes of Wrath," 1938–1941. Edited by Robert DeMott. New York: Viking, 1989.
Zapata: A Narrative in Dramatic Form on the Life of Emiliano Zapata. Edited by Robert Morsberger. New York: Penguin, 1993.

Autobiographical Nonfiction: Anthologies

The Portable Steinbeck. Revised, selected, and introduced by Pascal Covici, Jr. New York: Viking, 1971 (Contains "About Ed Ricketts," excerpts from *Sea of Cortez* and *Travels with Charley,* and the Nobel Prize acceptance speech.)
Selected Essays of John Steinbeck. Edited by Hidekazu Hirose and Kiyoshi Nakayama. Tokyo: Shinozaki Shorin Press, 1983. (In English with Japanese notes; includes "Making of a New Yorker," "A Primer on the 30's," "Jalopies I Cursed and Loved," "How to Tell Good Guys from Bad Guys," "My War with the Ospreys," "Conversation at Sag Harbor," and "I Go Back to Ireland.")

Autobiographical Nonfiction: Uncollected Articles

More extensive lists of this material may be found in Tetsumaro Hayashi's Steinbeck bibliographies, listed below.
"Always Something to Do in Salinas," *Holiday,* June 1955, 58–59, 152–156.

"Critics, Critics, Burning Bright," *Saturday Review*, 11 November 1950, 20–21.
"Critics from a Writer's Viewpoint," *Saturday Review*, 27 August 1955, 20, 28.
"Dubious Battle in California," *Nation*, 12 September 1936, 302–4.
"Duel without Pistols," *Collier's*, 23 August 1952, 13–15.
"Good Guy—Bad Guy," *Punch*, 22 September 1954, 375–78.
"High Drama of Bold Thrust through Ocean Floor," *Life*, 14 April 1961, 110–22.
"An Open Letter to Poet Yevtushenko," *Newsday*, 11 July 1966, 3.
"Random Thoughts on Random Dogs," *Saturday Review*, 8 October 1955, 11.
"The Secret Weapon We Were Afraid to Use," *Collier's*, 10 January 1953, 9–13.
"The Soul and Guts of France," *Collier's*, 30 August 1952, 26–30.
"The Trial of Arthur Miller," *Esquire*, June 1957, 86.

Autobiographical Nonfiction: Uncollected Series

"Letters to Alicia," *Newsday*, between 20 November 1965 and 28 May 1966 and 12 November 1966 and 20 May 1967.
The Louisville, Kentucky, *Courier-Journal* carried a series of reports on Steinbeck's trip to Europe between 17 April and 17 July 1957. No collective title was used.

Correspondence

Letters to Elizabeth: A Selection of Letters from John Steinbeck to Elizabeth Otis. Edited by Florian J. Shasky and Susan F. Riggs. San Francisco: Book Club of California, 1978.
Steinbeck: A Life in Letters. Edited by Elaine Steinbeck and Robert Wallsten. New York: Viking, 1975.

Novels

The Acts of King Arthur and His Noble Knights. New York: Farrar, Straus & Giroux, 1967. Edited by Horton Chase. (An uncompleted modernization of Sir Thomas Malory's *Morte d'Arthur*.)
Bombs Away: The Story of a Bomber Team. New York: Viking, 1942.
Burning Bright. New York: Viking, 1950.
Cannery Row. New York: Viking, 1945.
Cup of Gold. New York: Robert M. McBride, 1929.
In Dubious Battle. New York: Covici, Friede, 1936.
East of Eden. New York: Viking, 1952.
The Grapes of Wrath. New York: Viking, 1939.
The Moon Is Down. New York: Viking, 1942.
Of Mice and Men. New York: Covici, Friede, 1937.
The Pastures of Heaven. New York: Brewer, Warren & Putnam, 1932.
The Pearl. New York: Viking, 1947.

The Red Pony. New York: Viking, 1945. (First complete edition.)
The Short Reign of Pippin IV. New York: Viking, 1957.
Sweet Thursday. New York: Viking, 1954.
To a God Unknown. New York: Robert O. Ballou, 1933.
Tortilla Flat. New York: Covici, Friede, 1935.
The Wayward Bus. New York: Viking, 1947.
The Winter of Our Discontent. New York: Viking, 1961.

Short-Story Collection

The Long Valley. New York: Viking, 1938.

Plays

Burning Bright. New York: Dramatists Play Service, 1951. (Acting edition
    only.)
The Moon Is Down. New York: Viking, 1943.
Of Mice and Men. New York: Covici, Friede, 1937.

Filmscripts

The Forgotten Village. New York: Viking, 1941.
Viva Zapata! Edited with an introduction by Robert Morsberger. New York:
    Viking, 1975. (*Zapata,* listed above under autobiographical books, con-
    tains Steinbeck's original script for *Viva Zapata!* It differs greatly from the
    final film.)

SECONDARY WORKS

Only books useful for the study of Steinbeck's nonfiction are included. See *John
Steinbeck's Fiction Revisited* (Twayne, 1994) for a more extensive listing.

Bibliographies

DeMott, Robert. *John Steinbeck: A Checklist of Books By and About.* Bradenton,
    Florida: Opuscula, 1987.
French, Warren. "John Steinbeck." In *Sixteen Modern American Authors,* edited
    by Jackson R. Bryer, 1: 499–527; 2: 582–622. Durham, N.C.: Duke
    University Press, 1974, 1989.
Hayashi, Tetsumaro. *A New Steinbeck Bibliography, 1929–1971.* Metuchen, N.J.:
    Scarecrow Press, 1973; *Supplement I, 1971–1981,* 1983. Michael Meyer is
    updating Hayashi's work to 1996 for early publication by Scarecrow Press.
Woodward, Robert H. *The Steinbeck Research Center at San Jose State University: A
    Descriptive Catalogue.* San Jose: San Jose Studies, 1985.

Biographies

Benson, Jackson J. *The True Adventures of John Steinbeck, Writer.* New York: Viking, 1984. This monumental, more than thousand-page result of Benson's thirteen-year quest for information about Steinbeck pays more careful, discerning critical attention to the nonfiction and autobiographical fragments than any other available source. Benson provides an account of his research in *Looking for Steinbeck's Ghost* (Norman: University of Oklahoma Press, 1988).

DeMott, Robert J. *Steinbeck's Reading.* New York: Garland, 1984. A list of nearly 1,000 books that Steinbeck is known to have owned or read, annotated with many of his comments. Provides a unique guide to his acquaintance with nonfiction writing and his reactions to it.

Enea, Sparky, as told to Audry Lynch. *With Steinbeck in the Sea of Cortez.* Los Osos, Calif.: Sand River Press, 1991. A gossipy, illustrated account by the radioman on the *Western Flyer* that fills in much of what Steinbeck left out about the expedition with Ricketts to study marine life.

Fensch, Thomas. *Steinbeck and Covici: The Story of a Friendship.* Middlebury, Vt.: Paul S. Eriksson, 1979. Although the critical commentary is thin, the extensive quotations from Steinbeck's correspondence with his publisher/editor of most of the nonfiction provide more insights into the novelist's pursuit of an alternative career than any other source.

Hayashi, Tetsumaro. *John Steinbeck and the Vietnam War.* Part 1. Muncie, Ind.: Steinbeck Research Institute, 1986. No more issued. The founder and moving spirit of the International John Steinbeck Society presents from a sympathetic viewpoint what the writer came to regard as a personal and national tragedy.

Parini, Jay. *Steinbeck: A Biography.* London: Heinemann, 1994. Planned as a shorter biography than Benson's to be issued with a new edition of Steinbeck's writings, the book adds little to its predecessors and is more concerned with the major fiction than the works focused on in this study.

Steinbeck, John IV. *In Touch.* New York: Knopf, 1969. Most of this book is about Steinbeck's younger son's tangled career in the U.S. Army, but it is the only book in which a member of the family discusses personal relations with the writer.

Criticism

Most critical studies of Steinbeck's work are limited to his fiction. Only the most important comprehensive studies and books focusing on his nonfiction are described below.

Astro, Richard. *John Steinbeck and Edward F. Ricketts: The Shaping of a Novelist.* An analysis of the influence of the marine biologist and especially his nonteleological thinking on Steinbeck's career. Should be read in conjunction with Jackson Benson's biography.

————, and Joel W. Hedgpeth, eds. *Steinbeck and the Sea.* Corvallis: Oregon State University, Sea Grant College Program, 1975. The proceedings of a conference held in Newport, Oregon, 4 May 1974, with an emphasis on Steinbeck's relationship with Ricketts.

Coers, Donald V., Paul D. Ruffin, and Robert J. DeMott, eds. *After "The Grapes of Wrath": Essays on John Steinbeck in Honor of Tetsumaro Hayashi.* Athens: Ohio University Press, 1994. Contains Cliff Lewis's important "Art for Politics," essays on *Sea of Cortez, Travels with Charley,* and *America and Americans;* Susan Shillinglaw's "Steinbeck and Ethnicity"; and Donald Coers's long interview with Elaine Steinbeck about life with John. Also includes essays on the fiction.

Hayashi, Tetsumaro, ed. *Steinbeck's Travel Literature: Essays in Criticism.* Muncie, Ind. Steinbeck Society of America, 1980. Contains an overview of Steinbeck's writing on his travels by Richard Astro with articles on *Travels with Charley.*

Lewis, Cliff, and Carrol Britch, eds. *Rediscovering Steinbeck: Revisionist Views of His Art, Politics, and Intellect.* New York: Edwin Mellen Press, 1989. Papers delivered at a conference in 1986 to reexamine some of Steinbeck's less studied works and discuss the evolution of his artistic and social perspectives.

Millichap, Joseph R. *Steinbeck and Film.* New York: Ungar, 1983. A detailed history of Steinbeck's not always happy relationship with Hollywood and his own attempts at filmmaking.

Simmonds, Roy S. *John Steinbeck: The War Years, 1939–1945.* Lewisburg, Pa.: Bucknell University Press, 1995. A detailed account of a critical period in the novelist's life, with special attention to the reception of his writings in England.

Journals

Steinbeck Newsletter. Edited by Susan Shillinglaw, director of the Steinbeck Research Institute at San Jose State University, California. Has appeared semiannually since 1987, carrying short articles, reviews, and news about Steinbeck.

Steinbeck Quarterly (originally *Steinbeck Newsletter*). Edited by Tetsumaro Hayashi. Appeared quarterly or semiannually for twenty-five years (1968–93) as the official organ of the International John Steinbeck Society, founded by Hayashi to encourage Steinbeck scholarship by publishing articles, reviews, and news reports of interest to Steinbeck's readers. Publication was suspended following Hayashi's retirement as president of the Steinbeck Society in 1993.

Encyclopedia

Railsback, Brian, ed. *The John Steinbeck Encyclopedia.* Westport, Conn.: Greenwood Press, 1996. One of a series on major authors containing nearly a thousand entries on the subject's life, works, and influences.

Index

The Author

Warren French is an honorary professor of American Studies at the University of Wales, Swansea. He received his B.A. from the University of Pennsylvania and his M.A. and Ph.D. in American literature and history from the University of Texas–Austin. He taught at the Universities of Mississippi, Kentucky, Florida, and Missouri at Kansas City, and also at Stetson University and Kansas State University before becoming chair of the Department of English and Director of American Studies at Indiana University, Indianapolis, from which he retired in 1986. He is the author of three earlier books on John Steinbeck and of *Frank Norris, J. D. Salinger, Jack Kerouac, J. D. Salinger Revisited,* and *The San Francisco Poetry Renaissance, 1955–1960,* in Twayne's United States Authors Series. He was editor of the books on contemporary literature in this series and of Twayne's Filmmakers Series from 1977 to 1991. He also wrote *The Social Novel at the End of an Era* and edited four volumes on American fiction, poetry, and drama from the 1920s to the 1950s, as well as *A Companion to "The Grapes of Wrath"* and *The South in Film.* He was first president of the International John Steinbeck Society. He lives in Tallahassee, Florida.